A MAN, A MOP
&
A MILLION

To Linda,
You have such a
great family. You
are so Blessed. Your
looh awesome. Stay healthy
God Bless Always.
Love
Joey

A MAN, A MOP
&
A MILLION

A True Story of Humility, Failure, Success & Faith

Anthony F. Cimino

Contents

I	Growing Up Quickly	10
II	Earning and Learning My Keep	18
III	Marriage and Death	34
IV	Trying to Become Successful	40
V	No Time for Setbacks	46
VI	A Time for Giving	50
VII	A Test of Faith	54
VIII	A Precious Life	64
IX	Divine Intervention	75
X	The Celebration	82
XI	Giving to God	90
XII	A Humbling Journey	93
XIII	Nine Eleven	125
XIV	The New Move	147
XV	Know Your Strengths	156
XVI	The Mop	172

XVII	Just Say Yes	185
XVIII	Building a Business	198
XIX	Reality	203
XX	Bankruptcy	208
XXI	Rebuilding	213
XXII	Christmas and the Crash	219
XXIII	The Process	225
XXIV	Being Deaf a Success	229
XXV	Managing and Growing a Small Business	236
XXVI	Don't Ever Get Comfortable	239
XXVII	Offer More and Accept Setbacks	247
XXVIII	Cycles	250
XXIX	The Man, the Million, the Miracle	261
XXX	Our Dreams Come True	264
	God, Family, Giving Back	271

This book is an autobiography and a true story of actual events that were taken place by the author. Any incidents, names, characters that are mentioned in this book are not to shame, hold harmless, malice or slander. They are actual people who witnessed events that concur within the chapters of this book. The authors intent was to write a story to the best of his ability with truthfulness. Some content has been slightly altered to make the story more intriguing however, the basis of the novel is for the writer to show how negative events that happen in everyday life can be overcome by humility, truth, and most importantly, faith in our lives.

Acknowledgements

Mr. Jules Plangere & Family

Mr. & Mrs. Gerald Casper

Mr. Albert "Nubby" Napolitano

Mr. John Guinco

Prologue

To begin this story, you need to know that I am not a master writer, author, nor philosopher and I am definitely not a genius!

I am just a simple man with a simple story to tell. A story about life in general, and how it affects not just you, but everyone around you.

All of life's trials and tribulations. All of life's failures and successes. What is found, and of what is lost. The rich times we have in our lives and the poor times. The great decisions we may make and the decisions you never end up making. The friends and family that are presently here, and sadly, the ones that are not, and that you wish were still here with you.

This is a story of a simple life, a story of how things in life can get so complicated without a moment's notice.

My endeavor here, is hopefully, to spread some knowledge, experience, wisdom and faith, for all who read this book. I guarantee while reading it, you will have some tears of compassion, some tears of joy, moments of reflection, and moments of pain.

While reading my story, my aspiration is that some good will come out of it for you, so that your days ahead will be a little easier, and a little more simple, to help you get through the cycles of life that God presents to each of us every day.

May God bless you all, and I hope you will find my story worthwhile and invigorating to read.

Chapter I
Growing Up Quickly

Did you ever hear the story, my grandfather sailed across the ocean, came off the boat and landed on Ellis Island? Well, that was our family. And what do you think they did after they got off that boat? Well, they certainly didn't go to Disney World. They did what all the old school Italians did, they went right to work. For my grandfather, it was a vegetable stand in Brooklyn, New York. That vegetable stand marked the survival for my grandfather and a way to support his family. And so, the story begins.

For me, it started when I was young, growing up in the seventies. An old fashioned Italian home with my parents, two families and nine people living in same house and, of course, one tiny bathroom.

I was named after my dad. My dad, Anthony Cimino, Sr., was not a very tall man, but I remember him having biceps that looked like Popeye the sailor man. He had thick dark wavy hair and a very thin mustache.

My mom was a small, slender woman, with beautiful red hair. She was very soft spoken and would do anything for anyone. She was known for bringing homeless people into our home and feeding them dinner.

When I say two families lived in our house, I am referring to my brother and his wife and children. My brother Tom was a thin guy, with dark hair and also had that thin mustache just like my dad. Tom, his wife Carol and their three children would live with us occasionally. So, along with my sister, that made nine people in that tiny house.

At the tender age of five, I knew if I didn't get in that bathroom first, it would be next week before I would get in, especially with six females in the house. Realizing that, I learned if I needed to get something quickly, I would be the one running to get it.

At the age of six, my mom said to me, "Tony, you're going to be successful, responsible and learn to do things for yourself. Your father and I made a decision, and we are sending you to Our Lady of Mt. Carmel Catholic School." Man, do I remember that moment like it was yesterday. I may have only been six, but I certainly knew what I was in for, especially at Mt. Carmel! Suit and tie every day and where all your teachers were nuns.

Yes, I remember the first day very well. Crying in my dad's car for the entire fifteen minute drive. Screaming I don't want to go to school there! Let's be honest, no one wants to go to Catholic school, but it didn't matter, my parents were on a mission, and that mission was not to have another son come home with a wife, three kids and no job. Yup, that was the start of my life, and that's the way it was going to be.

One of my most vivid memories of Mt. Carmel Catholic School, was returning to class after recess. There was no playground for us to play on. We had recess in the parking lot. We had a lot of fun, playing baseball and other sports. However, when we returned to class, Sister Jacqueline would travel down each one of our seated rows and would place her finger behind our ear. If she detected any trace of sweat, and I mean *any*, it was a lunch detention for you the next day. Her reasoning was our parents paid a lot of money for our dress shirt and tie and we were not to get it dirty!

Unlike today, Catholic school back in those days was more like a military camp then a school and we all couldn't wait to graduate! Looking back however, it was just another way for our parents to enforce and embrace more responsibility and discipline into our young lives outside the home.

At the tender age of eleven, I had my first experience of true fear and this event affected my life forever. My mom, who played bingo regularly, was at her usual Tuesday night bingo game, and that left my dad at home with my sister and I. My grandmother was also living with us at the time. She was an awesome grand-mom! A real Italian grandmother, a little overweight, with a bun in her fiery red hair, always overlooking a pot of tomato sauce on the stove. She loved to cook, she made the best meatballs!

My dad loved having her home with us especially if he needed to go out on a call for work. At that time, my dad serviced old juke boxes, and pinball machines. Most of the calls would come from a bar or pub with a broken machine, but this night was a quiet night, and there were no calls.

On nights like this, we usually would both hang out to watch a Yankees game on TV. But this night was different.

In the middle of the fifth inning of the game that night, I went to go to the bathroom. On the back side of that bathroom wall, my parent's house had a sunroom, and it was where my grand-mom mostly stayed, watching her TV.

As I left the bathroom, I heard my grand-mom calling for me, "Tony, Tony!" I went to see what she wanted, and as usual, she was laying down on the sofa watching I love Lucy, her favorite TV show. She then says to me, "Tony, honey, can you go get me a glass of water?"

I answered her, "Of course, grand-mom." I went to the kitchen to get her a glass of water and as I go back and hand her the glass of water, she reaches out her hand for the glass, and falls off the couch.

My grand-mom was lying on the floor, right in front of me, face down and not moving! I knew something was terribly wrong because she wasn't responding to me. So I yelled and screamed for my dad! He came running to the back sunroom, and it was like, he knew what had happened. Then he started yelling at me to call 911 while crying over my grand-mom saying "Momma, I'm sorry!" over and over again, but there was no response at all from my grand-mom.

As I watched the ambulance drive off from the house, I knew my grand-mom wasn't coming back.

That night my grandmother died right in front of me. It was a massive heart attack from a blocked aorta in her heart. It was a moment in my life where I grew up very quickly, and it left a deep impression in my life for many years to come.

Time passed by and life slowly started getting back to normal again.

The following year I turned twelve years old, and at that time, I was already being groomed to work in my uncle's pizza joint called the Gold Digger. Back in those days, the "Italian" way was you were immediately groomed to work, either in a trade, such as plumbing, painting or even pizza making. And without excuses or questions, you were going to get a job!

The Gold Digger was a pizza shop Monday thru Thursday and was also a restaurant and bar on the weekends down on the Asbury Park Jersey Shore boardwalk. It was there, that I experienced my first knowledge of entrepreneurship.

The first lesson I learned was, when the boss, who happened to be my Uncle Nick, a big Italian guy, with tree trunk sized arms, says to you, this is where you're going to make pizza, then, you better know, this is where you're going to make the pizza! Understood Tony? My reply respectfully, was always, "Yes, Uncle Nick."

Then he says, "And another thing Tony, by no means do you leave this work area, not even to answer a phone, right?"

"Yes, Uncle Nick."

Then, my Uncle Nick says, "Good, then we understand each other!" It seemed like good advice my uncle gave me. But, at twelve years old, I had different ideas, especially seeing that my uncle owned the place. I mean, I'm like, I own the place too and no one is going to tell me that I can't take a break and walk around and have a soda, even my Uncle Nick, (who happens to be my dad's brother) I mean, that's unheard of right?

Big mistake!

So, the second day of work, my dad drops me off at my uncle's restaurant at eight a.m. in the morning, when its customary to start making the dough for the days run of pizzas. So before I start, I go get myself a soda in the back of the restaurant, which is what all twelve year olds do at eight in the morning. Then out of nowhere, I start to hear phones ring continuously in a room in the back corner of the restaurant. So, as a nosy little twelve year old would do, I decide to follow the rings where they were coming from.

I come upon a door in the back area, I open it, and see about ten desks, with ten phones, and ten guys on the phones wearing black suits with black hats. You know, those derby kind of hats you see in old black and white movies? As I look around in amazement, to my surprise, my Uncle Nick is standing in the back corner with this big old cigar in his mouth. When he noticed I was in there, he looks at me with this look of fire in his eyes, staring straight at me!

At that moment, two things entered my mind. One, either I'm not going to get out of here alive, or two, I'm not going to get out of here dead!

So my brain tells me to go back to my pizza station where I belonged at in the first place, thinking maybe I was protected by the dough there or something. But, we all know that wasn't going to work.

14

As time was going by, and I mean seconds, my thoughts were not to pee on the floor as I heard my Uncle Nick's heavy feet approaching the pizza station. I didn't have any time to think or have the time to get any words out of my mouth, and before I even knew what was going to happen, WHAM! The first hand slap of many came across my face! And then his words rang out, "Didn't I tell you **not** to leave your work station, Tony! Didn't I! Now, go call your father and tell him to get his ass back down here to pick you up."

I said to myself, that wasn't so bad, one smack in the face, and just call dad, this is pretty good. So, I go to the pay phone, luckily, I had a dime, because there was no way I was going into that room where all the phones were at to call my dad. I mean, I survived death once.

So, I call my dad, and explain to him how Uncle Nick got mad at me and hit me. Now, if anyone does not know Italian families, the last thing a brother of another brother wants to hear, is his son calling on the phone saying dad, Uncle so and so hit me. The next thing I hear before the click is, "Tony, I'll be right there, you stay right where you're at."

Well, the Gold Digger Bar and Restaurant, is about fifteen minutes from my house and my dad makes it in ten!

I then go to meet my dad at the front door and before I can get "Dad" out of my mouth, he has my uncle in a choke hold two feet off the ground against the wall! I hear my dad screaming at my Uncle Nick, saying, "You hit my son?" over and over and over.

My dad's choke hold was so strong, he wasn't giving my Uncle Nick a chance to speak and tell his side of the story. So at that moment, I sealed my own fate. I decided to go over to help my uncle and restrain the grip on my father's choke hold, this giving my Uncle Nick the chance to speak.

When my dad releases the choke hold, the famous words of fate had come out of my uncle's mouth, "Tony, I've been tryin' to tell ya, the kid, your son, he went into the back room!"

My dad's reply was, "He did what!"

Uncle Nick replied, "Tony, Tony, Tony, he went into the room!"

At that moment, a second stare of death was gazed upon me, only this time, from my dad! So, what did I do? That's right, I hightailed my ass back to the pizza station, because that was where I was supposed to be and I thought I would be safe.

It didn't take too much longer after that to get my second slap in the face, and my second command, this time from my dad. "Get your ass in the car, you don't work here anymore! You're a disgrace!" On the way home, I didn't say a word. I sat quietly while getting a tongue lashing from my dad, saying what a disappointment I was to the family.

When we got home, I ran into the house with two red marks on my cheeks.

When my mother saw me crying she asked, "Tony, what happened to you?"

Now, the last two times I answered that question, I felt pain, so I decided to keep my mouth shut and ran up the stairs to my room.

Upon my dad coming into the house my mother asked my dad what had happened. It got very quiet, then I heard someone coming up the steps. I thought it was going to be my dad to slap me again, but it was my mother, who dealt me the next piece of news. She said, "Tony, what you did today, is a lesson you will learn from, for the rest of your life. And that is, when a boss at your job, gives you an order, you better respect it! And when an uncle is your boss, and gives you an order, you better obey it! Think about what you did today. There will be no dinner for you tonight and tomorrow night."

Now, was this an intelligent price I had to pay for that kind of mistake, of course not, but at the time, this is what Italian families did. You grew up with only two ways of knowing, the right way according to them, and the wrong way according to them.

Chapter II
Earning and Learning My Keep

Soon after that, my dad thought it would be a better idea to put me into the "real" day to day work force. I was thirteen years old at the time, yup, that's right, thirteen and at another Italian Pizza Restaurant called Vic's. It's still to this day, one of the landmark pizzeria's on the Jersey shore, and remains a very popular spot to have dinner or a pizza.

In the summer of '72, I was hired by the owner, whose name was John Guinco. Mr. Guinco was a very nice Italian man, who knew my parents and decided to give me a chance as a busboy, cleaning tables after dinner. The job paid a $1.90 an hour. Now, that doesn't seem like much, but back in those days, it would get me to a bowling alley where I could bowl six or seven games, and play some pinball and billiards too.

Mr. Guinco was an excellent business man and person. He cared about his business and his workers. Many times, I would work the late shift on weekends and get done in the early morning hours. Instead of calling my parents to pick me up, Mr. Guinco would always find a way to bring me home, along with several other employees, in his 1972 Mercedes Benz. It was actually a cool thing to get a ride home from him in that car, and we were always very appreciative of him giving us a ride home on those late nights.

I learned a lot from him. He was a very patient man, stern, strict, compassionate. He was the kind of man that would always pick up the slack if someone needed help, whether it was the cooks, bartender, or the waitresses, he would always assist someone to make the night run a little smoother. I worked there throughout high school, at night, and over the summers.

I even worked at a bowling alley called Neptune Lanes. It was a great job. I mean after all, I was a bowler growing up, so why not? My job there was to work in the back of the alleys and remove bowling balls that got jammed in the back gutter of the lane behind the pins. Most bowling balls would get stuck there because of another ball jamming the door that releases the ball back to the bowler, down the front of the lane.

But what was great about that job was it turned out to be a great hangout for me and my friends. I remember, we had this room in the back of the alleys called "lane thirteen". It had a chair, couch and a TV set up in it. Some of my friends, once in awhile would bring their girlfriends there just to make out. All they had to do was bang on the back garage door to get in, it was awesome!

One night, I'm working there with my friend, Tom Casper, and he says, "Tonight has been real boring, what do you say we have some fun with the senior league that's bowling right now?"

I said, "Tom, what do you mean?"

"Half of them can't see, right?"

I said, "Yeah, so?"

He says, "Pick a real old guy out there, one you think can't see too well, but a pretty good bowler for his age."

I said, "Okay, got one, now what ?"

Then Tom says, "Take the stick that we use, the black one that looks like a fork, the one that we lift pins up with."

"Okay, got it"

"Now." says Tom. "Let's wait until the guy starts a new game, because we're going to take this stick and knock the pins down for him the whole game so that he gets a lot of strikes!"

I said, "What? They're going to see us!"

19

He says, "Hell no! Soon as the ball hits the pins, that's when I will take this stick and knock them down! I've done it before, don't worry, they won't notice. The back of the pin area, it's black too."

Well, after two or three frames, and three strikes later, we were laughing so hard because it was working! After about seven strikes in a row, people were starting to get excited that an eighty something year old man was throwing a perfect game! (That's twelve strikes in a row to all of you non bowlers out there).

Finally, when he got to the tenth frame, that's the last one in the game, we decided no more. It was starting to get serious. After he threw the sixth strike in a row people would stop bowling just to watch him.

On his tenth ball, he threw another strike on his own! Two to go and he has a perfect game! At this point, Tom and I are laughing so hard we were rolling on the ground.

Then he throws another strike, number eleven! Now, everyone gets quiet in the bowling alley and stops bowling to watch him bowl the final ball. Now we're thinking, if someone finds out what we did, we're fired.

Finally, on the twelfth ball, the last one of the game, going for a perfect game, the old man knocks down seven pins, and then receives a standing ovation! We started to roll on the ground laughing again, not believing what just happened! It was a night we never have forgotten.

Now, all of my friends, like Steve Eccles, Tom, his brother, Matt, and a lot more who were teenagers at the time, heard about what happened and wanted to work in the back of the alleys too. Each one of us were grateful to Mr. Napolitano who owned the alleys and decided to give us jobs there. It was a great way of earning money, learning mechanics, and staying out of trouble and to this day we all have great memories that we all share with each other from that job.

As for myself, at the time, I just took it as another way of saving money, bowling more, sometimes for free. Eventually, a few years later, I was able to buy my own car.

As I continued to work at both jobs, I became very close with Mr. Guinco and Mr. Napolitano. Both were mentors to me and I enjoyed every moment I spent with them.

I ultimately became bowling teammates with Mr. Guinco, the owner of Vic's Italian Restaurant. He always made time to talk with me about growing up, being responsible, and not taking anything for granted.

I became so close with him later on in my twenties, we both decided to team up together in a men's bowling league, and one year our team ended up winning the league championship. It was a great time in my life, and I'll never forget it. I owe a lot of my success to him.

As I mentioned, work was always going to be a big part of my life. During my years in high school, I would cut lawns, pump gas, shovel snow, anything to make a buck.

Meanwhile, back at home, things weren't going as well with my older brother, Tom. Unlike me, he was always looking for the shortcut to freedom and with three kids, that's not a successful way to go about things.

As I watched him, I continued to learn from him on what *not* to do. So I just decided to keep doing my own thing, and kept cutting lawns after school to make a few bucks.

I remember one day, after I was finished cutting two lawns, my buddies Matt and Joe, who were two years younger than me, called me at home and said, "Are you busy? Do you want to go behind the Getty station to hit some baseballs?"

Now, this Getty gas station they were talking about had a baseball field in the back of it, it was like our own little sandlot with a backstop fence to stop baseballs from going into the highway behind it. So I said, "Sure, I just got done cutting two lawns, let's go."

This day turned out to be my first encounter in life of really being in the wrong place at the wrong time.

We get to the ball field and Matt and I first grab our mitts and head out to the outfield, while Joe goes to the plate to hit some balls to us in the outfield. After about catching thirty or so balls, we usually would switch positions and now, it was Matt's turn to hit.

As Matt was running to the backstop area to hit next, three guys come up to me in the outfield where I was standing. One of them, I knew from my history class, his name was Leon. I'll never forget his name. He says, "Yo man", then grabs my arm and says, "Give me your wallet" and then proceeds to stick a pocket knife into my belly.

In shock I said, "Leon, what are you doing, you're in my history class man, for crying out loud."

He then said, "Shut the F*** up! I don't care about that s***, you know what, give me your money or I'm going to kill you man!"

As I go to reach for my wallet that had seventeen bucks in it from cutting two lawns, one of the other guys there kicks my legs out from underneath me, and the other one pushes me down to the ground and starts kicking dirt into my face.

That's when Leon grabs my wallet and says angrily, "He's only got seventeen bucks!"

Then one of them says, "Should I kill him now and put this knife in his gut?"

Needless to say, I was real scared now, fearing my life was going to end. Then for some reason, Leon shows mercy on me and says, "No man, he's in my history class,

22

just let him go." At that moment, I ran home as fast as anyone could. Luckily, I was pretty fast!

When I got home, my brother approached mc at the door and asked why I was sweating so much. I felt embarrassed about what had just happened, so I just told him we got done playing baseball and that was it.

The next day, I decided to visit my high school counselor and asked to be switched out of the class that Leon and I were in, and he complied.

About a month goes by, and for some reason I still don't know why, I never saw Leon again. He just vanished, and I was good with that, and I left it at that.

Thinking now, I probably wouldn't even be writing this book if I didn't have seventeen bucks in my wallet that day. I really believe they would of killed me. I figured I dashed a bullet, so I decided to just move on after that incident, and life was back on track.

Back to my older irresponsible brother. He would be working at Monmouth Park, a New Jersey horse racing facility, riding horses in the morning, doing workouts for trainers, and then taking the money he earned and betting on the first horse he liked when the track opened up. I watched this all go down as a teenager wondering, what was he thinking with three kids to feed and a wife to take care of, living in my parent's house.

One day, I remember he came up to me with this idea. He saw several older men working the crowds every day selling these "cheat sheets" at the front entrance of the track. Cheat sheets were type written paper flyers that would be sold for a dollar by professional race horse handicappers at kiosks when you first walked into the gate.

My brother took a liking to them and asked them one day if he could help sell sheets for them and learn the business. They gladly took him in and started teaching him how to work the crowds.

Soon after that, my brother bought a second hand printing machine. He put it down into the basement of my parent's house, with the approval of my father of course, because he was making money. He then started printing his own "Tom's Green Sheet".

He went back to the other handicappers, told them about it, and they offered him a position at one of the open kiosks. Things really started working out for him. He was so busy he even asked me to help.

As the customers poured in, he was working his kiosk station in the front of the track, while I had my own kiosk station in the back of the track, where the train loads of people would enter the back gates.

One day he asked me if I liked helping him do this. I told him, "It's ok."

Then he said to me, "What if I gave you a quarter for every sheet you sold for a $1.00?"

I said, "Sure, that would be great."

So, in the summer of seventy-four, at fifteen years old, I was bringing home about one hundred dollars a week. Not bad for a fifteen year old back then.

About halfway through the summer, I was really enjoying this new job my brother offered me. I knew it wouldn't last too long because it was just seasonal work, but I was working almost every day making decent money and I figured it was something my parents wouldn't mind because I was working with my brother, however, it wasn't going to last too much longer.

I remember one day, I came home, and out of nowhere my dad approached me asking if I was putting some time in at the alleys bowling. It seems, my mom told him I was nowhere to be found during the summer and he was curious about what I was doing with myself recently. What I didn't realize at the time was, my brother Tom, never told him I was working for him at the track.

I then found out my dad had some friends at the track who one day said to him, "I think your son is working at the track."

My Dad's reply to them was, "Yes, I do have a son working there, his name is Tommy."

"No, no, no." said his friends. "It looked like your younger son, Tony."

After my Dad shared this conversation with me, I knew where he was going. So, when my dad approached me on this, I told him the truth of course.

At first, he was actually happy my brother put me to work with him, but when I told him how much I was making, he was a little questionable about it to say the least. So, he asked me again, how much Tommy was paying me. I told him he was giving me twenty-five cents on every dollar sheet I was selling at the track.

When my Dad heard that, his expression was like, steam coming out of his ears! I said, "Dad, what's wrong?"

He said, "Your brother is giving you twenty-five percent? Looks like me and your brother are going to have a little talk when he gets home."

Now, every Friday night, my brother would walk into the door around seven o'clock. If he had a good day at the track, he would stay late and drop his sheets on the ground so that the next day, Saturday, the crowd would pick up the sheets off the ground and see how many winners he picked out of ten races, hence, him having a great Saturday day of sales.

This particular Saturday afternoon, he had a great day, selling almost five hundred sheets with five winners on the day. My dad knew this already from talking to his friends and figuring out, I should have at least one hundred twenty-five dollars for my work that day.

When my brother got home, my dad was waiting for him to show up. He asked my brother, "How much did you make today?"

My brother Tom, told him the truth by saying, "Five hundred dollars."

Dad then turned to me and said, "Tony, count your money."

When I counted it, I found out I only had one hundred dollars. Then my dad asked my brother, "Tommy how much money right now do you have in your pocket from today?"

My brother answered, "Not much, probably a couple hundred."

My dad says, "So, let me get this straight, you sold five hundred sheets for a dollar, cheated your brother out of twenty-five bucks and you only have two hundred bucks left in your pocket? So, where did all the money go son?"

My brother looked scared. My dad's face was a dead giveaway and it looked like he was going to kill him. The last thing you want to do in an Italian family is cheat your family out of money, so my brother answered truthfully and said, "Dad, I've been losing the money betting on the horses lately at the track and that is why I'm short money."

My dad's response was, while screaming at the top of his lungs, "Tommy, Tommy, Tommy! You want to screw up your life, that is up to you, and you got three kids home at my house you need to feed, but to cheat your brother out of his money!"

My Dad then went to his car and took a crow bar from the trunk, he proceeded down to the basement, and violently smashed the entire printing press into pieces, to the point it would never print again. I have never seen my dad so angry.

My mother hears all this commotion going on and now she gets involved. Normally my mom, would just keep quiet and tend to her business, she was a real sweetheart, but this day was not a day for that. She then comes running down to the basement screaming at my dad, yelling for him to stop. My dad then says to my mom, "This is it Tina, I'm throwing his ass out! He's a bum!"

Now, my mom would have none of this. She would get just as angry and yell back at my dad saying, "He has children and you will not throw any of my grandchildren out on the street!"

As I watched this all unfold, I knew of course, my mom and dad had been battling my brother's irresponsible ways for a long time. I knew at an early age this was not an acceptable way of life.

So, what did I learn from this? I learned under no circumstance do I cheat people. I learned to be honest, reliable and hardworking and don't ever take the easy shortcuts because they never work. This kind of behavior from my brother lasted for years, and every time I saw it, I saw the pain in my parent's eyes, and I made sure that I would never repeat his mistakes.

Yes, being fifteen years old, many vulnerabilities show up, some are never seen, but I figured some of it out. But what was really saving me at the time from my home nonsense, was a second family I knew growing up. They were the Casper family. The Casper's' lived just a few blocks away from where I lived. A great family; honest, religious, compassionate. They had three boys, two of them I spoke about already, Tom (who worked at the alleys with me), and his brother, Matt who I played ball with. The other brother was Mark, who was always in my homeroom in high school and was a great ballplayer. The brothers were all around the same age as me, plus they had one sister named Karen.

What I learned from Jerry and Rosemary Casper was money can't buy discipline. The Casper parents thrived on teaching their children discipline. There would be days I would go over there after school and on weekends to play basketball in their backyard. We would have great two on two basketball games. Occasionally, our other friends Tommy Caron and Steve Eccles would come over and make it a three on three. Those were great times.

There were other days where I would go over their house and I'd see Mark, the oldest brother raking leaves and his younger brother's, Tom and Matt helping. But that never stopped me from asking them, you guys want to play some ball today? On those days, they would look at me thinking I was crazy for even asking them! I'd say "What's up, common, let's go."

Mark's reply would be, "Listen, Tony, I don't know how it is at your house, but you see over here, if we stop doing what we're doing, we won't get our allowance money, and if that happens, we won't be able to go the alleys to bowl, shoot pool or even play some pinball. Here at home, we work for our money, and then we go to work at our own jobs and save it because some day, you see that mustang down the road, do you think my dad is going to buy that for me? So, if I were you, I'd turn around, and go get three other guys to play, because here my friend, we will be doing this for the next five hours."

And that's the way it was at the Casper house, and that's how I learned about discipline. I learned nothing comes for free, and the Casper family showed me that working at a horse racing track getting short changed from a brother who was gambling his life away, was definitely not the way to earn a living.

Learning from that, the next couple of years I bounced around working odd jobs like selling shoes, pumping gas, and I continued to work at the bowling alley.

Always saving my money for that car I wanted so desperately to buy.

By the time I was seventeen years old, I managed to save a thousand dollars and it was time to buy that 1977 Ford Maverick. But before I did that, I wanted to tell my mother about all the money I saved to buy that car. I approached her and said, "Mom, you're going to be so proud of me."

She said, "I already am Tony."

"Yeah, but I wanted to tell you, I saved up a thousand dollars to purchase my own car." I could see in her eyes how proud she was of me.

She then said, "That is so wonderful Tony. Do you know what kind of car you're going to buy?"

"Yes, a Ford Maverick."

Mom said, "Did you go to the dealer and ask the price?"

I said, "Yes, but I'm about seven hundred dollars short Mom, but I'm going to continue to save."

Smiling, my Mom then said, "You don't have to do that son."

"Mom, I'm not my brother, I'm not going to take anything from you for free."

My Mom motioned for me to come over and sit next to her. Then she said, "Tony, do you remember the thirty-five dollars I asked you for every month since you were thirteen years old, when you went to work for Mr. Guinco at Vic's?"

"Yes, of course," I said.

"Wait here for one moment," my Mom told me. Then she got up and went to her bedroom.

Upon returning, she sat back down next to me and said, "Well, I've been putting that money away in an interest savings account under your name at the bank." She then shows me a savings book. "Here is the savings book."

When I looked in it, there was enough money in there to pay for the car and then some. I asked her, "Mom, why did you do this?"

"Tony, as parents, you will find out you'll make mistakes, such is life, but it is very important that you learn from them. I told your father, we were responsible for the way your brother acts and treats you, so we weren't going to make the same mistake twice by saying, you don't have to work because you're too young. So, your father and I decided we were going to put you to work. Now, we didn't plan on what was going to happen at your Uncle Nick's place, but we were going to make sure you were going to learn responsibility. So, we opened up the savings account. We charged you rent, which we knew you weren't going to like but we knew some day we would give that money back to you, as a gift for being such a wonderful son. The money in that book is the money you earned respectfully and hard earned, take it, it's yours and go buy that car you want so badly. We're both so proud of you!"

I couldn't believe my mother and father would do that for me. I mean, when they were taking my money, I figured it was going towards bills in the house and to help my brother and his family. I was blown away.

I wanted to repay them in some way. I immediately went to see Mr. Guinco at Vic's Restaurant and told him what my mom and dad did for me.

His response was typical of him. It was why Mr. Guinco is one of the best men I ever met in my life. He said, "Tony, invite your parents over here for dinner, and I will only charge fifty percent of the bill, make the reservation and tell them I invited them."

I made reservations for them to have dinner at Vic's the following night.

When it came time to pay the bill, Mr. Guinco went over to my Dad and said, "What a fine son you have here. He told me the story about the rent, the dinner is on me."

My mom then started to cry, came over and hugged me and said, "You are a wonderful son."

That was a good night.

That September I started my senior year in high school and my bowling career was taking off. I always wanted to do well for my parents with bowling, because of all they did for me. On some days of practice, my mom would find the time just to keep score for me at the lanes after school.

I was having a tremendous year. I received numerous accolades and had many articles written about my accomplishments in the local newspapers. I received honors as being one of the best high school bowlers in the country, and my parents couldn't be more proud of me.

In the fourth week of the season, there was a bowling match between my high school, (Neptune) who was ranked #2 in the State of New Jersey and we were bowling against Brick Township High School, who was ranked #1 in the State of New Jersey.

It was a highly anticipated match between two of the best high school bowling powers in the state. A crowd of over two hundred people showed up for that match, and that is a lot of people to be watching a high school bowling competition.

During the second game of that match, my Coach, Amos Bass, approached me and said, "I see numerous bumps all over your body Tony. It looks like your getting the chicken pox, and unfortunately, I have to suspend you now from match play." I was devastated to say the least. It was the most important match of my life!

It turned out to be a horrible case of chicken pox that kept me out five weeks, and when there is only twelve weeks in the season, it didn't look good.

At the time, I was averaging a record high 207 for fifth highest average in the country and my goal was to win the State team championship and to be named to the All-State Team. Needless to say, the state high school provisional bowling rule requires you to have four weeks or twelve games bowled in a season to be eligible and recognized for National Honors.

Well, it wasn't until week eleven I returned back because of more devastating news in between. In week eight, I was diagnosed with the Hong Kong flu, and not only did we lose our state ranking, but my scores and season ended up being disqualified for the year, and that was it.

All the practicing, all the hard work, all the time I put into my season came to an end. I was disqualified from any National Honors, and collegiate offers. My ranking and awards and any scholarship I was set to receive were gone.

This was so upsetting not only to me, but to my parents as well. Financially, they were not very stable, almost poor. My brother and his family basically soaked up every dollar my parents earned and they made it very clear to me, if there was any chance of going to college, it would have to be through a scholarship, so my season ended, along with my dreams of going to college.

After that, my senior year was continuing and moving along and I understood the only way I was going to make a life for myself was to get out there and work after I graduate. Bowling was gone and a scholarship was not an option. Having that attitude wasn't unfamiliar to me, as I had been working my entire life.

I immediately got a job after school selling shoes, and working again at a gasoline station pumping gas on weekends.

When graduation came rolling around, my dad came up to me and said, "Tony, I understand you're working two jobs however, gasoline and shoes are not the kind of jobs that will get you what you need the rest of your life." College life wasn't in the plans so, I figured he was right.

My mom was very proud of my accomplishments as well, knowing how hard I worked and the effort I put into my bowling career. She decided to throw me this sensational graduation celebration where two hundred fifty out of five hundred high school senior graduates showed up. It was the best party ever!

After that night, I knew how much I meant to both of my parents, I also knew when it was over, it was time to get on with my life. It was time to get a real job.

The following week, I decided to visit a local bank, New Jersey National Bank in Asbury Park, and put in an application. I figured a banking job was the best way to go. I was good at math in high school, had great recommendations, and I knew a couple of people who worked there.

No sooner than a week goes by, they call me, and offered me a lower level position rolling coin for them. You know, all that loose change from the Laundromats and public parking meters, it all had to get rolled in wrappers, counted and deposited into their personal or business accounts. It was a start, but like I said, it was a lower level job, and it got my foot in the door, and without a college education, I figured it was okay.

Chapter III
Marriage and Death

Soon after rolling coin, I turned twenty years old, and my experience from that first bank job paid off. I then landed a job at First Merchants National Bank, a more prestigious statewide bank that had career incentives and a retirement plan. It was there, as a loan collector, I learned how to deal with people in desperate times and then at the same time, be dealt with my own hardships.

Two months into my job, my brother gave me awful news that no twenty year old would want to hear, and I will never forget that conversation. I found out from him, not my dad, that our mom had cancer. Just like that, my mother at fifty-one years old, had been diagnosed with stage IV Hodgkin's Disease.

Now, it wasn't like I never heard news like that before, remembering when I was eleven, my grandmother died right in front of me. So, upon hearing the news about my mom, for some reason, I was in denial and the news didn't seem to bother me. Maybe being eleven years old at the time, and seeing the sudden death of my grandmother, or just a combination of that and feeling moms don't die young, whatever the reason, it didn't seem to deter me from my job, bowling, or meeting my future wife, Darcy at work. So, I kind of put that news in the back of my head and continued my work as if everything would be okay.

As a loan collector, I learned you really need to separate your problems in life so you can deal with others who have different problems, sometimes worse than your own. You learn how to talk to people who can't pay their bills, and in conversation you try to manage a way for them to pay them without consequence, only problem for them is, there has to be a consequence. Bottom line is, you have a job to do, and that is to collect money from them, for their furniture, personal reasons or car loans. In automotive cases, you have to repossess their car if they can't pay, it's that simple. And always, without fail, they were the best cars to go repossess, usually Camaros, Firebirds, and even Trans Ams.

When I first got this job, I was introduced by Human Resources to Mr. Ed Zieser, a ruthless, bastard of a manager you would never want to meet or work for! Man, was he tough, a proud six foot five grey haired German who resembled Hitler on his best day with a temper that would make Hitler even proud.

He would oversee you with a client on the phone to the point where you never wanted to get off that phone without getting a promise of payment from that customer. It was either you get the money, you get the car, or you get fired! There were no excuses to be made.

Coming from a tough Italian heritage background like myself, I knew exactly what he wanted, and I knew how to give it to him. My expertise with people and their problems made my job easy. I would listen to customers on the phone and their problems and show compassion for the jobless, the illnesses, and for the deaths in their families. In some cases, I would compensate them a month not to pay for a nominal interest fee and in the same conversation, let them be aware that I have a job to do, and if they can't pay their car two months from now, I'm going to be over their house to take it. Most times they would understand and comply, some would lose their car, but either way, my negotiations with people really impressed Mr. Zieser. So he decided to promote me to Assistant Manager of the collections department at the young age of twenty-one.

It was here at First Merchants Bank where I met my future wife, Darcy. She worked in the Installment Loans department right across from me.

I knew Darcy in high school and we ended up getting the job at the bank at the same time. We began dating and after a year, I proposed to her. It seemed we were a perfect match. While we were dating, we both were able to relate to family tragedies. I feel this was the most defining part of us and our relationship and it really brought us closer together. We had a real understanding and compassion for each other.

We both lost our grand-moms at an early age, and she knew about my mom's cancer issues, but what I never expected to hear from her was that her oldest sister had breast cancer. I was seriously upset over hearing that news. Michele, who was twenty-three years old at the time was diagnosed with stage II Breast Cancer and it ended up being the toughest time of our lives. We both had a new job, in love, a serious relationship evolving, a sister seriously ill with cancer and a mom who was dying of Hodgkin's disease. Two twenty-one year olds, thrown into a web they have never seen before.

We decided to get married and set our wedding date. At that moment my thought was, I wanted my mother to be around to see me get married, but in the process, Darcy's family was upset over the timing, because they just found out Michele's breast cancer metastasized to her liver, and it immediately put her in stage four terminal cancer. Michele had been going through such rigorous chemotherapy treatment for two years.

Back then, chemotherapy was in its early stages and the treatment from it caused so many complications. Michele, fought incredibly hard with all the treatments she was receiving. The news was devastating, but it didn't deter Michele, she was a fighter and during this time she married my brother-in-law to be, Lenny. It was a beautiful wedding in a park, on a gorgeous sunny day but everyone knew the news wasn't great on the forefront.

There was a noticeable change in her stomach with the liver expanding from the disease, it looked like she was nine months pregnant. Turned out, it was the fluid starting to build up in her body and we then realized she only had a short time left to live.

In July, four months before our wedding date, I approached Darcy and asked her if she wanted to move our wedding date up because Michele was getting so sick. Darcy's family was against that idea, instead, they turned around and said, maybe we should cancel the wedding completely because now is definitely not a good time.

Under normal circumstances, I would most certainly agree, the last thing you want to do is rush into a marriage with family turmoil surrounding the event, especially a daughter or a sister with terminal cancer. But as I said, my mother was dying too, and the last thing that was going to happen on my end, was for me to call off a wedding when probably it was going to be the last event my mother was going to attend in her life.

Darcy and I seriously discussed the situation, and made a decision to keep the date, November twenty-second, Nineteen Eighty.

On September twenty-third, two months before our wedding, my future sister-in-law Michele Easterling Bode passed away of metastasized breast cancer at the age of twenty-five. The next two months after that were gut wrenching to say the least. The family was obviously in mourning and going through a very difficult time. A mother lost her first daughter, two sisters were scratching their heads wondering how this could happen, the father was nowhere to be found, (he just divorced Darcy's mother a few of years before), and a new husband was in shock and in a depression over the loss of his wife.

Plenty of reasons to cancel a wedding. But as I said, for myself, it was about my mom and Darcy understood that, as she was close with my mom too.

After many family discussions, and many crying days, Darcy's family agreed to put this very sad day behind them, for at least a couple of hours of happiness and decided to keep the wedding as scheduled.

As for my mom, on my wedding day, fortunately she had a bounce back from her chemotherapy/radiation treatments and was able to attend our wedding. I even got to dance with her, and sadly, turned out to be the last dance I had with her. For the next six months, the cancer started to invade her lungs, and like Michele was having a hard time breathing from all the chemotherapy treatments and radiation therapy. Her weight went from one hundred fourteen pounds down to sixty pounds, and every day I saw my mother for the next six months she could no longer get out of bed.

I couldn't believe this was happening again, and to my mom.

On the night of June twenty-third, nineteen eighty-two, I watched my mother take her last grasps of breath, like I watched my grand-mom, and my sister-in-law Michele. They were the longest last breaths I have ever witnessed of someone's life. Every last one gave me so much pain in my heart, like none before.

After a two year illness, my mother quietly passed away of Hodgkin's lymphoma cancer. At the time, I never ever, thought that would happen. I was devastated. I remember the talks so well with her in the bedroom as she was fighting for her life. She used to remind me all the time, be strong for your family, love your family, and above all things, love God. We had talks about growing up, being a hard worker, being an honest human being, and always keep caring for people. She always said, "There's always going to be obstacles you'll have to overcome, there's always going to be people who have worse problems than you, and there always will be family there for you to take care of. You must not remove God from your life! He is the only one who will get you through the obstacles and turmoil, no matter how tough they may be, so don't ever lose sight of that."

I made sure I never did. That night, I learned death is such a permanent, final event in someone's life and it is so powerful it effects so many. My feeling to this day and always was, you can't do what you do dying, so do what you can do living, at least that's what my mom and dad taught me.

That's what Darcy and I continued to do, live!

The first round of deaths were over, a grandmother, sister and mother, all of whom we patterned our life after.

Back to work we went. We got our first apartment and four years later had our first child, a son, Michael. It was then I said to myself, it's time to step up to the next level. Better job, better home, better husband and now a father.

Chapter IV
Trying to Become Successful

After we had our son, Michael, I get a call from my father-in-law and he says, "I have a potential job consideration for you. I happen to know the owner and publisher of the Asbury Park Press Newspaper. I see him almost every day, and we were talking about you. I thought maybe it might be a good idea for you to visit the Human Resources department first thing Monday morning and mention my name. You just might be interested in getting a job there."

I said, "Okay, thanks. Sounds like a good idea."

The Asbury Park Press was a highly touted newspaper in the area, and a job everyone wanted coming out of high school or college. I didn't mention anything to Darcy about her dad calling me, it just happened to slip my mind at the time.

A few days later, we were sitting at the dinner table and she spews out, "You know, my dad works at the Asbury Park Press, and I heard from him there were a few openings in the pressroom. You know a lot of people over there, why don't you give Harry Carlson, the Pressroom Manager a call?"

Well, right then and there, I'm thinking, never turn down a possible job offer from your wife's dad, especially if he mentioned it to you already once before, and now he mentioned it to his daughter. Most importantly, it was a career job, with great pay, and benefits.

We both felt this job opportunity could possibly be the most important career decision in our lives. So after two interviews, I came home to my wife Darcy and shouted, I got the job! She was ecstatic. We both knew this was a great job opportunity and our lives would be financially so much better, especially with a newborn son to raise.

I started out at the bottom position as a paper handler. My responsibilities were unloading trucks, taking out the trash, and setting up for the next day's paper run, hoping someday to become the next foreman of the plant. It was great on the job training.

I learned mechanics, advertising, sales, printing, all facets of the newspaper, and I knew one day it could possibly lead to a management position. It was also a trade job, something from back in my youth that my father talked to me about. He always said, "Remember Tony, if you can't go to college, the other way to make a living is through a skilled trade position," and learning how to print a newspaper was a great way to earn a living. Best thing about the company was longevity and security. The newspaper was family owned, and in business for over 135 years!

Everything seemed like a perfect fit. I just had my son and now I had a career job. But just when things started to settle in, another obstacle was put into place. Little did I know how serious it was going to be, but it was a big part of my life and I knew it could be a life changer for me.

As I mentioned before, the sport of bowling happened to be a very important part of my life, as a youth, and growing up into an adult. I'd been practicing and playing competitively since I was seven years old, and I did have aspirations one day of making it to the professional bowlers tour. I never, ever dismissed my bowling talents. I always stayed in shape, still practiced two, three, four times a week, bowled in leagues regularly hoping someday I could make a career out of it. Even with having a son, and a full time job, I continued to pursue something I loved and knew I was very good at. I kept bowling in leagues, entering tournaments and even trying out the pro-am circuit bowling tour with professionals like, Marshall Holman, Mark Roth and Johnny Petraglia, from Brooklyn, New York to name a few. All members of the bowling Hall of Fame now.

With a raise in salary on this new job, it made it easier for me to enter into some tournaments. Some of the fees ranged from fifty dollars to five hundred dollars, but it was well worth the risks with the talent that God had given me, so why not try.

In the summer of eighty-three, a year before our son was born, I was having a great year and getting my name out there by qualifying in some highly competitive tournaments. But at the same time, it seemed bowling scores were on the rise, and I was having a tough time competing at that level, so I decided to ask other good bowlers around on why this was happening and I got my answer.

It was called the new "finger tip" grip that was making the difference. The equipment, approach and style of the game was changing and that was making scores go up rapidly. The new trick was to put as little of your middle fingers into the ball as possible, so that when the ball releases off your hand, the last thing that will come out of the ball was your fingers. No longer was the thumb hole a necessity into your shot. The result was more rotation on the ball as it rolled down the lane, which would give the ball more power to plow through the head pin causing more action on the pins. Resulting into more strikes and higher scores.

I quickly moved to have this change done to my bowling ball, and after a couple of months I was able to raise the level of my scores back up to the level of others. Back then, the pro bowling tour required sanctioned league bowlers to maintain a one hundred ninety average for thirty-six consecutive games for two years straight in order to obtain a PBA Card (Professional Bowlers Association) and I was on my way.

I had a new job, new family and things were really looking up. So I continued to bowl, and bowled well. So now after a year went by and the birth of our son, I felt I was ready to enter into some highly competitive tournaments.

One day, after work, I called Darcy and asked her if it was okay to get some extra practice in. It was the week of the Monmouth County Masters Tournament, a tournament that strictly caters to competitive skilled high level bowlers in the state, and I wanted to get ready for it. She knew how important it was to me and said, get as much practice as you need.

I felt pretty good that day, but I noticed my hands were more sore and swollen than other days and I figured it was from some extra work I had to get done at the newspaper. That day we had a lot of paper rolls to push around and they each weighed about five hundred pounds, but I gave it no thought, and I bowled anyway.

It turned out to be one of the worst decisions of my life, and the final day of my competitive bowling career.

As I said before, there was an equipment change, and the object was to release the ball from the fingers with extra "lift" to get more revolutions on the ball for a more powerful result.

It was about the sixth game of practice, I normally bowl ten to twelve. I went to the approach, put my thumb in last as always and proceeded to walk "for the delivery". My backswing felt good, my arm had a pendulant swing as always and then the weirdest thing happened, at the release point, I felt my thumb come out of the ball, but my fingers slightly stayed in longer than usual.

The next thing I heard was the loudest "pop" you ever heard from a human hand, and the harshest pain you could ever feel. I went down screaming as my ball continued to roll down the gutter.

Mr. Napolitano, owner of Neptune lanes and my coach, (he used to be a professional bowler in the forties), was there to witness what happened and knew all too well what the results would be.

He ran down from the counter area, after hearing the "pop" and said it looked serious! What he saw was a complete separation and tear of the third and fourth ligaments of the middle and fourth finger. My fingers were limp, swollen, and I had no feeling.

He immediately ran to the concession counter in the back, grabbed some ice out of the fridge, applied a bag of ice and wrapped a towel around my hand to relieve some of the swelling. I looked up at him and asked him those fatal words, "Am I done?"

He almost started to cry and I knew that was it.

For the next six weeks, I was in a small finger wrap cast because I still had to go to work. A year later, after I had healed, I tried to comeback but unfortunately the hand wasn't strong enough to support the weight of the ball. My bowling career was over.

I realized then, you never know what time is your time, with anything. Your life, sports playing, job. It can happen at any moment.

But I always lived by one thing, failure is not an option, in anything, what you don't succeed you must try, try again, even if it is something else. In my case, I had a great wife, a wonderful son with a great job and I still had a house on the horizon to buy, so there was no time to weep, moan or cry about this.

It was time to renew my thoughts, goals and agenda and put what had happened in the past once again, behind me, it was time to move on, get focused again on new responsibilities and a new life, without bowling, it was time to get back to work!

Chapter V
No Time for Setbacks

My main job, at the Asbury Park Press was to start working at three in the morning to get the newspapers out, this way the customers had them on their driveway to read before six a.m. The last paper we printed came off the line usually around ten in the morning. Then, for the next couple of hours you clean the presses, then yourself and by twelve you're finished with your shift.

One day at work, a friend of mine, Gene Lewis, approached me and said, "You know after work, I clean a post office in Allenhurst. (Allenhurst is a small town on the Jersey Shore) and I heard Spring Lake Post Office is looking for a cleaner. I thought you might be interested."

I said, "Thanks Gene, I'll check it out." I figured, with the extra time I had without bowling in my life anymore, this was a great opportunity to put some money away for that house we wanted to buy one day. Turned out to be a great move, because right after that, we found our dream house and we were able to buy it.

Our home was in a quaint small community named Neptune City. It was the next town over from where we grew up and had a population of about six thousand people. Neptune City had parks and playgrounds, baseball fields, and a wonderful pizzeria called Pete and Elda's. It was just what we were looking for!

When our son turned five, we enrolled him into kindergarten at Woodrow Wilson elementary school, and I was immediately asked by some parents if I wanted to get involved with the Board of Education, Town Council, or some other public volunteering function.

I figured I was always involved with sports all my life, so why not get involved with the Board of Recreation. I was well known in the community with my bowling career and used to play baseball in high school. By getting involved with my community, I could get to meet some really good people, and public volunteering is a great way to make a difference in your home town.

For the next couple of years, I found myself working with police, fireman, and public works. We even went to the Mayor's Ball. It was there, where I first met Mayor Robert Deeves. Mayor Deeves was a long time Mayor in Neptune City who did wonderful work for his community. He approached me that night at the Mayor's Ball and asked me how I liked the programs I was volunteering in, and wondered if I would be willing to do more with kids. Well that was easy for me, I said, "Absolutely Mayor."

Mayor Deeves decided to make me a Recreation Director of the town and said, with my knowledge and people that I know, he would give me the freedom to implement any programs that I could come up with to enhance the youth, the playgrounds and the recreation of our town. I thought this was a great opportunity.

In nineteen ninety-two, we had our second child. A beautiful baby girl, Marissa Christine Cimino. We gave her my mother's name as her middle name. She had the best looking eyes you ever want to see, and she had lots of energy too. You know, the ones that wake up every hour of the night, crawl out of their crib, can't sit still in a stroller in the mall, you know what I mean. She was a true blessing for us, and we really felt our little family was complete.

Three months later, our joy and happiness was suddenly overshadowed by fear.

Darcy's mom was admitted into the hospital with a 99% blockage in both of her carotid arteries. Her surgery was set for Wednesday, however that morning there was a back-up in the operating room and her surgery was delayed until the late afternoon.

While she was in the hospital, they had her on a blood thinner, Heparin and the morning her surgery was scheduled, they took her off of it completely.

It was about three in the afternoon when we walked into her room, sat down for about ten minutes, and noticed in the middle of talking to her, she was going in and out of conversation, then all of a sudden her hands starting trembling and then she started complaining about a vicious headache.

I immediately went to chase down a nurse in the hallway, got her into my mother-in-law's room, and then all hell broke loose!

The nurse runs out of the room and starts yelling in the hallway outside the room, Stat! Stat! Stat! over and over and over. They came running into the room with crash carts and we were abruptly pushed out of the way.

About an hour later my wife, Darcy, her other sister, Kathy, myself and her brother Brett were approached by staff and led into another room down the hallway to hear the news we all dreaded.

Her doctor said to all of us, your mother had a cerebral hemorrhage and a brain stem bleed, she is in a coma, and will never come out of it, there are only two options.

Hearing this news we were all numb, it was supposed to be a basic operation, home in two days. I then remembered the feeling of losing my mom, and I never wanted to see this family go through such a horrific situation like this. I said to myself, how God, is this possible? A woman comes in for a somewhat standard operation in a hospital and doesn't come out?

A few hours went by, talking to doctors, talking amongst ourselves, the moment was surreal. And then the decision by the family was made to take her off life support.

Frances T. Easterling died moments later at the age of sixty. A wonderful woman, mom, and grandmother. And just like that, our new little daughter lost her only grandmother.

Darcy and I were only married twelve years at the time when this happened. This meant, by the time we were thirty-two years old, we had both lost our moms, grandparents, and a sister. It's a tough thing being so young, losing close family members.

We discussed this situation seriously and came up with one conclusion, God needs to be in our lives more than ever now. We knew He is the only one to seek when it comes to life and death moments, and He is the only one that will help comfort you in your pain, restore your soul and strengthen the love you have in your heart when a crisis enters into your life.

After Darcy's mom's funeral, we both decided it was time to get back to church on a regular basis which we so much needed.

We always went to church of course, Baptisms, Confirmations, regular Sunday mass, the usual, but it was time to get more involved with God on a personal level, we really both felt that way.

But it was also a time again to focus more on work at the newspaper, the post office cleaning job and the Mayor wanting me to head up the recreation program. I had decided at this time in my life, that when a death occurs in a family or even a close friend, the best way to overcome sadness and depression was to get right back to work and start focusing on the good things in life even more.

Chapter VI
A Time for Giving

While working at the newspaper I got to know and became close with Mr. Jules Plangere, owner and Publisher of the Asbury Park Press.

Mr. Plangere was a self made millionaire who took a small family local newspaper/radio business and turned it into one of the most profitable well known media businesses in the country.

Mr. P., as I referred to him, was always an employee friendly type of guy. He used to get up early in the morning, and by six a.m. he would enter the pressroom just to mingle with a few of his pressroom employees.

He kind of reminded me of the movie actor, Charlton Heston, an older gentlemen with a big heart. He had a way of making us all feel important, always saying to us pressman, "The pressroom is the last thing on the line to building a newspaper and the most important." He always used to say, "If it weren't for the ink, no one could read it!"

Every once in awhile I used to bump into him in the hallway and we would always have a conversation about something, business, sports, life, he always took the time out to talk.

I remember back then, I used to run a company picnic once a year for all the pressroom shifts. Always on a Sunday, because most of the weekend newspaper was printed and done by five a.m. Sunday morning. Our picnic included three games of softball where all the shifts and its employees and families would come to participate, eat and play.

Before the event started, maybe a week before, I would collect five dollars off of everyone who was scheduled to play and put it towards hamburgers, hot dogs, beer and condiments for the day. All the families would come, eat and watch their family members play in the three softball games. Usually, about two hundred to about four hundred people would show up, and we would all have a great time.

One year, on the Monday morning after our picnic, my boss Al comes up to me and says, "Tony, Mr. Plangere wants to see you in his office right now, no questions asked."

I said to myself, I hope to God I didn't mess up on an advertisement that I printed the other day because whenever Mr. Plangere wanted to see you in his office, it wasn't good. So, after Al came up to me, I immediately went to his office and his secretary called me in.

Mr. Plangere then said to me, "Tony, have a seat. There's something very important we need to discuss."

Somewhat nervous, I said, "Okay."

He then started talking about the company picnic and wanted to know how long I had been organizing it. I told him about four or five years. He then wanted to know the cost of it, and I said, with all the food, ball field and miscellaneous expenses about a thousand dollars. He then said, "The reason why I brought you in here Tony, was for two things, and two things only."

My mind was racing left and right, trying to figure out if I was going to get fired or suspended without pay for some reason. Then he asked, "How many people attend this function on a Sunday in July?"

I said, "About four to five hundred people Mr. P."

"Let me ask you Tony, I assume these are my employees right?"

"Yes sir, and their families."

"I was wondering, these employees were invited, right?"

"Yes." I said, wondering where Mr. Plangere was going with this.

"Well, don't you think I should of been aware of it or notified about it too?"

Immediately I said, "I'm sorry Mr. P., I should have advised you."

"Then why wasn't I invited?" he asked.

I then stared at him in amazement and didn't know what to say. He then asks, "I hear you took some money off of them, correct?"

Now I'm thinking I'm definitely fired. He must of seen the fear in my face because the next thing out of his mouth just shocked me. He says, "Tony, relax! I'm just busting your chops! However, from now on, for every year you intend to do this function, I want you to visit me first in my office a month before the event, this way I can give you a check for one thousand dollars, and I don't want you to collect another cent off of anyone anymore for that day."

I was like, wow! Not only did that relieve me, but impressed me and surprised me just as much. I didn't know what to say to him other than thank you Mr. P.! Mr. Plangere then said, "If anyone asks you about this meeting, you just tell those guys in the pressroom, you're all doing a hell of a job, and let them know the reason why you were here was because I was proud of your color work with the Macy's advertisement in the Sunday paper."

Still stunned I said, "Okay Mr. P, your words are safe with me." I then left his office thinking this man didn't want anyone to know of his gesture.

I then thought about a scripture in the bible saying, "Give without repayment and expect nothing in return." I was blown away by his generosity.

I then went back to work and I told the guys exactly what he told me to say, and true to his words, every year after that, he would call me into his office and give me a one thousand dollar check for the entire day's festivities.

I learned a lot from Mr. Plangere that day and from that moment on, I wanted to instill his compassion, generosity and philosophy into my life completely.

Chapter VII
A Test of Faith

With the sudden death of Darcy's mom, we both felt Marissa was a gift that God bestowed on us, to ease the pain and loss from losing her mother. However, before we could get comfortable with the idea that maybe life might shed some long lasting happiness without another sad event in our family, we were immediately tested once again.

One summer night in July, just after we put Marissa to bed, the phone rang. It was Darcy's older sister Kathy. She was hysterical on the phone, and had to be calmed down.

Her gynecologist noticed something unusual in her blood work that day, and because of her first sister, Michele dying of breast cancer, there was an immediate response by the doctor to have a mammogram done.

Upon receiving the results, the news was confirmed. Kathy was diagnosed with the same cancer her older sister was diagnosed with, breast cancer. The cancer was stage four and it had to be dealt with immediately.

Kathy underwent a bi-lateral mastectomy with immediate reconstruction. Her oncologist recommended aggressive chemotherapy. The only problem, Kathy was not very fond of the chemotherapy protocol because it didn't work for her older sister, Michele, who died at twenty-five years old and went through the same rigorous chemotherapy sessions.

I can recall Kathy noticing the pain and discomfort her sister was going through and used to say if I ever get cancer I would never go through the treatment plan my sister went through.

Kathy felt the chemo accelerated Michele's death even more. Now, Kathy, thirty-four at the time, had other plans of treatment to fight the cancer. So while she was being pro active in her own way, we were dealt with another new blow to our own immediate family.

One Saturday morning, after a pancake breakfast, of course it was always, "Dads delicious pancakes," our daughter, Marissa, who loved Mickey Mouse, would sit down and watch her favorite TV channel, which was the Disney Channel. She loved Disney, and enjoyed all the characters, so as any parent would do, we accommodated her and allowed her to watch without resistance.

While she was watching her favorite show that day, I turned to her and said, "Maybe when you get older, we'll take you to see Mickey Mouse's house. Wouldn't that be great?" She would immediately perk up, and get excited when we mentioned Disney to her. Darcy and I used to talk about going to Disney World all the time, so this gave us an excuse to go. After all, with the sudden death of Darcy's mom, we thought it might be a good idea to just get away. We couldn't ignore the commercials on the television anymore saying, you need a little magic in your life, come to Disney World!

So we figured, why not. Kathy was dealing with her cancer and was finally getting the treatment she desired, so we decided to get away for a week.

A few days later, while driving in the car with Marissa in the backseat, I decided to bring up the conversation again saying, "We're all going to Disney World soon to see Mickey Mouse!" Now, usually when I did that, I would get an overwhelming response of approval from her, a scream, a laugh, something. Only that day, it didn't happen. So I said it again, and I spoke louder this time. I don't know why, I just did.

Again I said, "Riss, we're going to Disney World!" Again, no response.

I then looked at Darcy and said to her in a quiet voice, "Do me a favor, turn to Riss and say to her in a normal tone, we're going to Disney World."

Darcy then turned to face Marissa and said, "We are going to Disney World."

Just as I expected, a big "Yay!" came out of her mouth.

After that, Darcy, in a louder voice, yelled at the front window saying again, "Can you believe we're going to see Mickey Mouse!"

No response at all from Marissa.

We both looked at each other with fear and anguish. We knew something was seriously wrong. The rest of that day we were purposely and intently testing her in conversation to see if she was hearing us. We would cover our mouths and talk with her, we were going into other rooms and calling her, and even standing behind her asking questions like, "Do you want to go to bed now? Riss, do you want to play outside? Are you hungry?" Nothing.

We feared that day our daughter had a hearing issue. To what degree, we didn't know but we didn't want to jump to any conclusions. However, we knew something was wrong.

We quickly decided to make an appointment with an Audiologist, Dr. Sandy Kuhn in West Long Branch, New Jersey. She was highly recommended by our pediatrician, Dr. Bogdan of Neptune, New Jersey and he thought it would be best to research and diagnose Marissa's condition even further.

On the day of her appointment, Dr. Sandy, as everyone calls her, invited us in along with Marissa to explain exactly what she looks for when someone is experiencing a hearing loss. Her examination that day was all about tones, decibels and sensory, then finally placing a

56

headset over Marissa's ears to detect how much of a decibel loss she was experiencing.

After her tests were completed and the results finalized, she concluded there was a mild to moderate hearing loss and recommended that we visit Children's Hospital of Pennsylvania (CHOP).

We immediately made the appointment and within a week, we were scheduled to meet with the pediatric doctors on staff in the Pediatric unit for hearing impaired children.

We arrived there in the morning and soon after a meeting with staff, they escorted Marissa into a sound proof room, where they did testing. After the consultation and testing, we met with the doctor and our worst fears were confirmed. Our daughter was hearing impaired and had sensorineural nerve damage.

We asked the doctor, "What is sensorineural nerve damage?"

He went on to explain to us how during the pregnancy, the nerves in the inner ear did not fully develop. He told us they have no idea why this happens, but in some cases, as time goes by, the patient may continue to slowly lose their hearing and become completely deaf. He told us, unfortunately, there's no way of telling if Marissa's condition will worsen. But he did say, it will never get better.

The doctor advised us that our daughter will have to be closely monitored until she reaches the age of twenty-one, because with this type of condition, she could lose her hearing completely.

As soon as we heard that diagnosis, Darcy and I both looked at each other thinking the same thing, we've been through so much, and now tragedy has struck our child.

We asked the doctor, how do we manage this, no one in our families are deaf, and no one knows how to do sign language. We don't know anyone with this condition. We were utterly devastated. We didn't know the first thing on how to handle this disability.

The doctors there were great. They noticed we were extremely emotional and they calmed us down. They said to us, there are many programs out there that can offer assistance for your daughter, such as speech therapy, exceptional hearing aids, and sign language. The way to beat this is the same way you beat an illness, you become pro active and learn how to speak for her, learn to advocate for her, and attend speech and sign language classes with her.

We listened to their advice intently, and we immediately responded into action So, at the tender age of three, when she was diagnosed, we were quickly able to get her into speech therapy sessions, to help with her disability.

During this time, we received other devastating news.

Kathy, Darcy's second sister took a severe turn for the worst with her illness. She chose to fight the cancer without chemotherapy and that was failing her now and her prognosis wasn't good.

We knew her health was going to worsen quickly because we didn't feel her choice of treatment was the right choice, so we decided to quickly book that Disney vacation we were talking about, and enticed Kathy to come with us. We thought it would be a good idea at the time to spend some quality time with her, and to get her away from all the negative news that was surrounding all of us.

After about two days into the vacation, she unfortunately started to complain about severe, vicious, headaches. We tried to convince her to cut the vacation short and get back home to the doctor as soon as possible, but Kathy didn't want to leave. Unfortunately her condition continued to deteriorate and we all decided to cut our stay in half.

When we returned home, we quickly rushed her to the doctor's office and had the necessary tests completed.

After two days of impatiently waiting, the results showed her cancer had metastasized into the brain and central nervous system and there wasn't much they could do. The news was devastating for all of us, especially to our son, Michael, who was extremely close to his Aunt Kathy.

After hearing the news, he was having a hard time with this as well, understandably so. He was only ten years old at the time and already had lost his grandmother, his sister was going deaf, and now his favorite aunt was very sick and dying. I tried having talks with him, but it was just too hard for a ten year old to understand. I knew that, because I had been in that situation before.

Soon after that Disney vacation in February, the inevitable happened. It only took two months for my wife to lose another sister to cancer.

Kathy Easterling died at the young age of thirty-seven. That made two young sisters dying of breast cancer, each choosing a different course of treatment.

After hearing the news, Darcy's gynecologist, who was also Kathy's gynecologist, Dr. Grimm of Neptune, New Jersey called her and suggested that for the next few years she should have thorough examinations done to prevent this disease from attacking her. Dr. Grimm also suggested that Darcy have a prophylactic surgery to remove her breasts, but she declined that idea.

This really hit us hard, knowing another death of a loved one so young, and another pain in our heart to endure. And a third sister wondering if this was going to happen to her too. You can't help but think what might come next, but like I've said before, you must turn to God, for hope, peace, comfort and faith during these times. He is the savior of our lives and we must show confidence in what He teaches us. We were steadfast on this thinking and time and time again He was always there, in our hearts, in our minds, and in our soul to help us manage and cope with the worst of our tragedies.

About a year later, I remember my son, who was eleven years old at the time, started asking me questions like, why is all our family dying, dad? Why is it always cancer? Is this going to happen to mom too?

Frantically, he said, "Dad, I'm in sixth grade now and at this rate it seems no one in our family is going to be living to attend my high school graduation!"

I told my son, Michael, "All you can do in life is control your own destiny. We don't have the power of God, but we do have the control and brain power to make our own decisions, and to be responsible with the choices we make in our own lives. That is what God gave us, freedom of choice and free will. Hopefully, someday, we will have answers to the questions you just asked me. The most important thing to remember is this, we have our mind, our soul, our faith, our heart and they are the core gifts of what God gave us, and it is up to you, to use those resources to do astounding things with your life. We all have a life to live, and whether it's for twenty years or one hundred years, God gives us the body and the mind to use, and not to abuse, so use it well son. That's the best advice I can give you right now."

As I remember back then, that was one of the toughest talks I ever had with my son, but I couldn't let that moment get away from me. I had to show him I had strong faith and belief in God, maybe not all the answers, but hopefully through my faith and his, my son could find a way to accept what has happened.

After Kathy's death, we really had to get back and focus on our daughter, time for her was of the essence. She was only four years old and Dr. Sandy was saying there's no telling when her hearing may get worse.

Next on the agenda for Marissa was to get her in a school for hearing and speech disabilities. At the time, we had no intentions of mainstreaming her into a regular school, but we also realized she somehow managed to have a "gift to communicate".

Her speech and hearing therapy sessions were going well. The technology of the hearing aids were getting better, and her lip reading was extraordinary! She was using sign language consistently and thriving with it.

I'll never forget one day, I was in the garage lifting weights, doing my normal exercise routine and all of a sudden she did one of the most amazing things you hear about, but never see. I was on the flat bench getting ready to lift the bar up and I see her placing parking cones around the perimeter of our garage. She was only six years old at the time. I said to her as she read my lips, "Riss, what are you doing?"

She then puts one finger up at me, (sign language, meaning to wait) grabs the basketball in the corner and starts to dribble the ball around the cones without stopping. Around and around she went, bouncing that ball in between the cones. I couldn't believe what I was seeing! I said, "Riss, how did you learn how to do that?"

Using sign language, she said, "Dad, everyday in the gym at school I do this, I love playing basketball."

I then said jokingly, "Well, hello WNBA!"

Around this time, my son Michael, was playing recreation basketball at his grammar school in Neptune City.

One night, I went to watch him play when Kevin Kenny, and his wife Louise approached me. Kevin and

Louise Kenny were directors of the recreational basketball league at Wilson School, and they did not want to direct the program anymore. They knew how involved I was with the community and the kids in the town so they asked if I was interested in directing the league. They told me there were about two hundred boys and girls who play in the program and all I would have to do is watch the gym and make schedules for the referees, games and coaches. It seemed pretty simple and worthwhile to me, so I accepted their offer and took this opportunity to enhance our community.

I then met up with a young man who was coaching a boys team there. His name was Michael Skudera. He was about fifteen years younger than me and he had a lot of energy in him. He seemed really mature and positive and wanted to be more involved with our town. So I asked him if he would like to be my assistant. He was thrilled and thought it would be a great opportunity. Then I asked Mike, "Do you have any ideas that would enhance the league?"

His response turned out to be one of the most fantastic ideas I've ever heard from someone that young. He said, "Tone, why don't we have an All-Star Jam night for this community? You know, like the NBA does on TV every year?"

Excited at that thought I said, "Mike, that's a great idea!"

We then decided to organize it, choreographed it, promoted it, and it turned into a TV show. It took almost six months to design the show.

Our main goal every year was to showcase the police and fireman and have them play in a shortened length basketball All-Star game. It really brought the community together.

We combined it with audience participation with events like three point shooting contests, raffle giveaways, free throw contest, etc. A lot of effort and work went into preparing for this one night, months in advance. I would send letters out to major sponsors such as, professional sports teams, major companies, even small businesses in the county asking them to contribute.

All the proceeds from the show would benefit parks and playgrounds, kids programs, and sports programs in our community. Sponsors such as the New Jersey Nets basketball organization, the New York Knicks, and the Milwaukee Bucks all participated by sending us memorabilia, signed jerseys and balls for prize giveaways.

I couldn't thank all the volunteers enough for their hard work, time and effort over the years they contributed towards this event. It was by far the most rewarding, satisfying endeavor I have ever been involved with my entire life.

Chapter VIII
A Precious Life

This was a great time in my life because not only was I helping other kids, but I was spending valuable time with my own. My son, Michael was already established in the school and I was helping Marissa with her basketball playing abilities.

By the time, she was seven years old and in third grade, she was playing with ten year old boys. At ten, she was playing on an AAU twelve year old girls team named the Howell Lady Rebels.

We knew she was special, but this was very encouraging. She was adapting and accepting her hearing disability while playing a sport she loved, and she was quickly learning how to handle her impairment in a positive way. It was a moment in our lives that was very exciting and rewarding for us, and we were seeing rapid results.

As life was moving along, it really wasn't time to get to comfortable yet. Another health challenge presented itself, only this time it hit too close to home, and this one was the most devastating.

Late December, early January was the time of year when Darcy and I would always look forward to scheduling a family vacation to Disney World in Florida.

It was January, nineteen ninety-seven and as usual, kids were out of school for Christmas vacation, so it was time to take our yearly trip.

We head to the airport, park the car, have breakfast and get on the plane to Disney. It was a beautiful cold winter day but we were all saying we can't wait to get there, because it was going to be eighty degrees.

We arrived at our hotel, the Disney Wilderness Lodge, a Magic Kingdom resort, at noon. We settled into our room, then headed out to the pool.

Yes, it was eighty degrees and it was beautiful out. Darcy and I decided to have a pina colada at poolside, while the kids had a snack and then we all went swimming. That night, we went to dinner at our favorite place in the world, Chef Mickey's.

Chef Mickey's is an extraordinary popular stand out buffet at the Contemporary resort hotel in the Magic Kingdom. Prime rib, baked Alaska, Chicken Marsala, you name it, it was on the menu. We met a wonderful waitress there too. Her nickname was Sunny, how appropriate! In our opinion, she was the best server there. Year after year, we would always ask for Sunny because she was such an awesome young lady and was really great with kids.

During dinner, it was a very festive atmosphere. Napkins would be waving in the air to the music played every half hour and that's when Mickey's cast of characters would always stop by the table and sign autographs and take pictures with the kids. It was a wonderful time.

That night after dinner, the kids wanted to go back to the hotel and swim in the pool, and of course, we accommodated them, we were on vacation! We left Chef Mickey's, went to our room to change, and headed out to the pool area for the night.

Michael, my son, who was thirteen at the time, was very thoughtful and offered to watch his little sister in the adult pool, while mom and dad went into the hot tub. The night was going as planned and we were having a fantastic time until we stepped into the hot tub. What took place in the next few moments would change the course of our lives and our family, yet again.

As I turned to Darcy to say what a beautiful night and hotel we're at, I saw this look of fear on her face like I've never seen before. I said, "Honey, what's wrong?"

She didn't say anything. She just took my hand and placed it over her right breast above her nipple, and I immediately felt a lump the size of a marble. It was the most defining thing I have ever felt in my life. We both looked at each other and knew exactly what it was. There was no doubt in our minds, and then the words came out of Darcy's mouth, "I have cancer, I know it." We both started to tear up and were stunned that this could happen again.

We then composed ourselves because we didn't want to let the kids see us upset, after all we were on vacation, and that was the last thing we wanted our kids to see.

I said something to her I will never forget, "You're not dying on me!" It just came out. "I'm going into the lobby and I'm going to call Delta Airlines right now, we're out of here tomorrow."

I then went to the Hotel Concierge and asked him to get the Hotel Manager. I told him it was a personal matter and I needed to discuss something with him that was very serious. He called him right away. The manager then came over to me and I told him the story of what happened in the hot tub and I also filled him in on the family history. His next words to me was something I needed to hear, "If there is anything I can do for you Mr. Cimino, call the airline, call a taxi, your luggage, please anything, I will do it.

I started to tear up, my emotions were getting the best of me. He then brought me into a room, got me a soda and said, "Here is your bill" and he ripped it up right in front of me. He said, "Mr. Cimino, you go make the airline changes, I will have my concierge bring your family a little something to the room, like pastries and coffee." He then said, "You're probably not going to get a flight out tonight so rest up in your room. In the morning when you wake up, breakfast will be on us. When you are ready to leave, see me and we will figure out when your family is going to come back here again for a better vacation, courtesy of the Disney Wilderness Lodge Hotel."

I was floored! I said to him, "Disney is Magic!"

He then said, "Go and get your wife better. We will see you again in the near future." I couldn't thank him enough.

As I was walking back to the room, I started thinking how I was going to tell the news to our kids. I started to remember those talks with my mom, her always saying, there are going to be times in your life with crisis, despair, failure, anxiety and fear. Those are the times you will need to call on God, and ask him for guidance, patience, compassion and love. It is those moments where you must be responsible, understanding, straight forward and tell the truth without regret or second guessing.

I then had a sense of a calm that came over me, like my mother was guiding me through this nightmare. I experienced a wave of strength, and a power of patience like I never felt before. As I walked into the room, I said to Darcy we need to tell the kids everything before we get on that plane. I don't want to hold anything back from them, right from where we're going, to what were going to do and no matter what, give them the strength, confidence and calm knowing we got this, and tell them you're going to be okay. Darcy agreed.

At the Wilderness Lodge, there's this wonderful fireplace in the main lobby. It's about seven stories high and its billowing fire heats up an atrium the size of a basketball court. It has multiple wooden rocking chairs in front of it where you can sit down and have a coffee, relax and watch the fire. This is where we decided to have our talk with our kids.

It was about ten a.m. that morning and we were getting ready to leave. The hotel concierge saw us there and came over to let us know our flight was on time, so we had plenty of time to talk.

Our son, who was in eighth grade at the time made it easy for us. He said, "What's going on Dad, why are we leaving? I know something's wrong, parents don't pack luggage one day later after they get to Disney World. Is it you mom, what's wrong?"

I could see the fear in his eyes, and then it came out of his mouth, "Mom, you have cancer don't you."

Darcy said directly to him, "Yes Michael, I'm pretty sure I do."

Michael asks, "How bad?"

"I have a lump on my chest."

Angrily, Michael said, "That doesn't mean you have cancer Mom!"

Darcy goes over to him and hugs him. "Michael, let's get this out of the way right now. Normally, anyone who finds a lump, really doesn't know what to expect but as for me, because of our family history, things are quite different. Your Aunt Michele died of breast cancer, your Aunt Kathy died of breast cancer so I'm not going to sugarcoat this news to you by saying, don't worry about it or lie to you. Now, does that mean I'm going to die of cancer like them? I can't answer that question, however, your father and I have been up all night talking about the way to attack this disease, I unfortunately inherited. And today is the first step of many we're going to take to fight it."

At this moment, I couldn't believe the courage and resolve this women showed me. She had so much strength, faith and confidence. There was no feel sorry for me. It was something I'll never forget, and the kids took the news just as calmly, just as if they missed a basketball shot. It was like, everybody hands on deck, go get'em MOM!

I was relieved. Her talk made my talk so much easier. All I had to say then was okay let's go get some breakfast and kick some cancer butt!

At that moment, the Hotel Manager came over and said to us, we can return again anytime your mom's ready to come back.

That afternoon, we got on the plane and headed home.

Once we got home my first job was to go tell Mr. Plangere at the newspaper what was going on. He immediately brought me into his office without hesitation and asked what the plan was for Darcy's treatment. I told him Darcy was on the phone making appointments with the necessary doctors and that we were going to attack this disease head on. He said, don't worry about anything else just get her better. All I want is your permission to call you up at home once in awhile to see how she's doing. Again, I was blown away by Mr. P's heart and generosity. I left calm, collected, and a sense that everything was going to be okay.

The next thing on my list was advising our community since I was very involved as a member on the Board of Education, the Recreation department and directing basketball and youth operations.

My first visit was to my Assistant Director of community basketball operations, Mike Skudera. I told Mike about Darcy's condition. I said, "Mike, we came home early from our Disney vacation and I wanted to explain to you what was happening."

As I was speaking with Mike about Darcy having cancer, he started to get really upset. He knew about our family history, and he immediately gave me a hug and said, "I'm here for you pal, your community is here for you, and the people of Neptune and Neptune City will be here for you. Go get Darcy better and don't worry about all of us here, will take care of everything on our end."

I said, "You're the best Mike, and I will stop by the gym from time to time to see you. I'll need to come here just to clear my head and get a breather once in awhile. I have already seen what this disease has done to so many people, so I'm sure there's going to be some rough moments."

Mike then assured me it was time I get some help and stop worrying about always giving it. He said, "Tony, there are many people in this community who love you and your family. We're all here for you, don't worry about anything. You were here for me when I needed knee surgery, I'm here for you now."

That talk with Mike made me feel great. I knew he was going to be mature enough to handle the direction of the program while I was gone.

The next thing I did was call my close friends, the ones I grew up with as a kid. The Casper family, Rosemary and Jerry and their sons, Mark, Matt and Tom, the guys I used to play basketball with everyday when I was young. I also spoke with my best friend at the newspaper, Gene Lewis.

I called them for support, because I knew I was going to need it. Truth be told, I had the faith and the confidence, but my realistic side was always playing games and trying to get the best of me. My feeling was, I could be a single dad one day, and if that happened, I needed people to be there for me and my family. After all, there really wasn't much family around anymore.

So I called them all personally, and separately and told them what kind of friends they were to me all these years, and how important they were to me and my family. I knew I had always been blessed with the best core of friends, so when I told them about the news they all told me they were here for me, anytime, day or night. And they were true to their word, whenever I needed a break, a babysitter, or even a night out for a beer, they made sure they were there for me and my family.

After consulting with Darcy's gynecologist, he recommended a couple of breast surgeons. We did our homework, looked at their experience, practice and knowledge. Darcy then chose, Dr. W. Dean Adams of the cancer surgical team at Jersey Shore Medical Center, Neptune New Jersey.

Dr. Adams was a young looking doctor with excellent credentials. Upon meeting with him we felt comfortable and confident in his abilities and the way he presented himself and he really impressed us by his compassion. It seemed he really cared about his patients and the concerns they had about surgery and life after surgery.

On January seventh, nineteen ninety-seven, we had our consultation with Dr. Adams. During the discussion with him he made it very clear that there was no time to waste, it was time for action. He then said to her, after reviewing your x-rays, mammograms, and MRI'S, your treatment plan for surgery and after will be an aggressive one.

Darcy asked Dr. Adams, "What does that mean?"

Dr. Adams then responded, "For some women, I would recommend a lumpectomy, however, in your case, I would not advise that. With your strong family history, I would not even suggest a partial mastectomy, but a bilateral mastectomy. You may not like that scenario, especially you Tony, but I want you both to understand something. I am here to save your life!"

My response to him was simple, "Do what you need to do Doctor Adams."

He then said, "Tony and Darcy, this is how we're going to proceed. Because of both your sister's history, an aggressive cancer has to be treated with an aggressive treatment plan. Our first step is to remove your breasts, and I'm going to suggest you have your ovaries removed as

71

well." Dr. Adams looked right at me and said, "Tony do you understand what this means?"

I replied, "Yes Doctor, no more children."

Then I said, "Dr. Adams, just save her life, that's all I care about."

"Both of you get some rest, your surgery is scheduled for January fifteenth, eight days from today," Dr. Adams told us.

When we came out of his office, we were stunned. I wanted to cry, but my heart and head was there for Darcy, so I hugged her and said, "I love you. Let's attack this and get started on it quickly. I got the rest of my life to live with you and this is only getting in the way of it, besides we got kids."

I then went back to work at the newspaper for a few days and tried to resume life as normal as I could, picked up the kids at school like always, went to my board meeting at town hall like always, and took a couple of visits into the gym to see Michael play basketball. On those nights, I always received hugs from everyone who was involved with the program. People like Cindy and Dan Gorman who were scorekeepers for the league, Bill Kroll and Bob Temple and Chuck Mitchell who were referees, and of course my Assistant Director Mike Skudera. All of them wishing us well and saying don't worry, the community has this all under control.

So, my homework was done, everyone knew what they needed to know, and it was time to face cancer head on with the most important person ever in my life.

The day before Darcy's surgery was January fourteenth and she was admitted into Jersey Shore Medical Center at two o'clock in the afternoon. I remember it like it was yesterday. I stayed there all day and into the early evening with her, having lunch, dinner, ice cream and watching TV in her room.

Darcy's cousins, Maryanne and Suzie were home with our kids, so I knew everything was okay at home, but it was an exhausting week for me.

I didn't want Darcy to realize how tired I was and at that moment, she turned to me and said, "It's ten o'clock, you look exhausted, I need you to be rested, I need to know you're going to be okay, and I need to make sure you can handle the family. So I want you to go home now, get some rest, the surgery is set for seven a.m. I will see you in the morning."

I felt like, wow, what this woman is going to go through tomorrow and she still has the strength to make me feel like she's so under control.

I went home crying in the parking lot that night as I walked to the car, not knowing the outcome of tomorrow.

As I headed home, I feared the kids were up, and I certainly didn't want them to see me in this condition, so I had to compose myself quickly.

As I walked in the front door, the first words out of the kid's mouths were, how's mom? I said, no worries guys, she's ready. Then Suzy gave me a big hug and left, while Maryanne stayed over for the night knowing I had to get up early.

I cried myself to sleep that night, only to wake up at three in the morning with the worst anxiety attack ever. I immediately took a shower hoping to calm down, then had a bowl of oatmeal and bananas. But that still couldn't get rid of my shakes, as many times as I tried to pull myself together I couldn't. I was talking to my mom under my breath hoping some way through her spirit she could calm me down. The more I tried to relax, the more I was getting nervous. There was nothing I could do. I then grabbed my wallet, my keys and left the house.

I got into my car, opened my door, got in and closed it. Sitting there thinking, it didn't take long for me to lose it. I started to cry profusely. I had my open hands on the steering wheel and my head buried in my hands.

I started to ask my mom for help, then Darcy's mom, her sisters too, then I started to pray to God, saying this prayer:

Dear Lord, I know you have so much to worry about, and so many things to handle, but please, I am begging you like I never begged you before, please, I never asked you for much, money was never important to me. But my mother was, my grandmother was, Darcy's mom and sisters were, please if there is nothing I ask off of you in my life ever again, please give me something, some sign, something to show me my wife Darcy is going to be okay. I will owe you the rest of my life for it!

Immediately at that moment, right then and there, may the Lord strike me dead, if this miracle in my life never happened...

Chapter IX
Divine Intervention

While praying my prayer request, my head and face were buried on the steering wheel while I was crying and praying, then all of a sudden I looked up.

Out of nowhere, the biggest, brightest headlights I have ever seen on a car came on! I looked at my headlight switch, and it was off! I made sure my car wasn't on, it wasn't. I looked for any sign to show me if I hit any automatic buttons. I didn't.

But the overwhelming thing of this intervention, and it was an intervention, no doubt about it, was my anxiety had completely left my body! It was like, I took a couple of Advil to get rid of a headache, and it went away in two seconds!

But the other thing was, I felt an inner strength of comfort and calm, an inner peace, and a feeling that whatever happens, God is in control of Darcy's life. I sat back in the seat amazed. I then started my car. Immediately the headlights went off. I then pulled the switch on the headlights, and my headlights went on.

I then drove to Dunkin Donuts to get a coffee and arrived at five a.m. at the hospital.

I proceeded down the hall to Darcy's room, and of course, when I saw her, immediately told her what had happened. She joked with me saying, it was a dream. She looked into my eyes, and she then realized, I was really telling the truth. She started to cry happily.

The head nurse came into the room and asked me what I had done to make her so upset. Darcy immediately told her the story and the nurse gave us both a hug and started to cry too.

It was time for surgery, the nurse told Darcy, okay honey, kiss your husband, time to go to sleep, time to get you better. Her words only made me feel more confident of Dr. Adams, the hospital, and his staff.

After about five cups of coffee and a three hour surgery, Dr. Adams approached me in the waiting room and said what I wanted to hear, "I think we got it all Tony, everything went great! We took some extra lymph nodes out as a precaution, but I don't feel there will be any lymph node involvement. Pathology reports will confirm that with me today."

I must of hugged him for five minutes. Dr. Adams then said to me, "Now comes the toughest part. First you need to know your wife's body is not going to be the same, we've had talks about that, but this is real. Second, she needs your reassurance about family, all Darcy was concerned about was you and the kids. Let her know you have everything under control. Next, when she gets out of the hospital, as I told you, in our first consultation, because of her family history she will be undergoing some of the most rigorous chemotherapy ever. Dr. Greenberg, and I have determined the treatment which will consist of Adriamycin and Cytoxan, every three weeks, with two weeks off in between. The effects from these drugs will cause nausea, mouth sores, weakness, loss of appetite, loss of hair and loss of energy. This treatment is what is going to save her life, but you need to be confident in the doctors because it's going to be a very stressful time for Darcy's body, and everyone who's around her."

I said, "Doc, you know how I feel about her, I'm there."

When Darcy was out of recovery, and in her room, I immediately was there. I noticed all the bandages around her breasts and asked her if she felt sore. Her reply was, "Do you think they have good ice cream here" I was like, wow, this woman is unbelievable. I kept saying thank you God, over and over again.

A few days went by and her reports were good, so the doctors decided to send her home. I prepped the kids with everything that was happening and they were great about it.

The following week we had an appointment with Dr. Susan Greenberg, Darcy's oncologist. It was time for her first round of chemotherapy. Dr. Greenburg invited us both into her office and explained the side effects to us again, but in a confident matter of fact, professional way. Like this is what I do and I do it well, sort of way.

She starts Darcy on her first IV drip and we're on our way. During that procedure we were talking to Dr. Greenberg, and she made it very clear to both of us that Darcy's appetite should be conservative, bland and not to over eat. She was worried about the reaction from the chemotherapy.

After finishing her first treatment, which only took a couple of hours, Darcy was feeling pretty good. She was hungry and wanted to eat at her favorite place for dinner, TGIF Fridays. My response to her was, are you sure you're up to that, I mean you heard Dr. Greenberg, maybe go get a salad, but Darcy said, hell no, I want to eat!

My mind, was saying confidently, no should of been said, but the words wouldn't come out of my mouth. So Darcy orders a New York strip steak, baked potato and a vegetable and I get the same. The food was delicious, and dinner went really well.

The night went well too, until about three in the morning. That's when Darcy started continuously to throw up, uncontrollably and left me no choice but to get her to the hospital. Immediately, after being admitted, the next person I see in the room is Dr. Greenberg, and the first words that came out of her mouth were like flaming fire torches being directed at me! She says, in a loud voice, "What the hell happened to her?"

I then explained to her what Darcy ate, and then she says to both of us, "I don't know who's responsible for this, but I thought I made it very clear yesterday. A light bland diet for her, after every treatment. Do you both know what happened here? Never mind, I'll tell you what happened here, she got poisoned. It's not a good idea to put red meat in your intestines after I administer your chemo treatment, understood?"

I was like, geez, this doctor really cares about her or is she just having a bad night. But at the time I'm thinking, who am I to question her, so I kept quiet.

After a couple of days at the hospital, we drove home, and Darcy rested for the next two weeks before her next treatment. I then was able to take some time off and that gave me family time to play with the kids, bring them out to a couple of basketball games, etc. I wanted to give them the security to know everything was going to be fine.

The next chemotherapy treatment came soon enough and this time we were figuring it would go better, but that unfortunately wasn't meant to be. The insertion of chemo went well, and everything looked to be normal for the first couple of days, but as the week went on Darcy mentioned to me her mouth and throat felt like it was burning and everything she ate and drank tasted a little weird to her.

After the first chemotherapy and what had happened I didn't want to take any chances, so I called Dr. Greenberg and told her of Darcy's complaints. While talking to her on the phone, she assured me that this was normal, but to keep an eye on it and to call her if it worsens.

Now another problem was, Darcy was worse than me when it came to making everyone think everything is fine, and that was not the way to handle this situation, especially after what happened last time.

After complaining about the sores in her mouth, I asked her if it was okay to bring the kids out, and she assured me everything was fine. As I said, at the time, I wanted to make the kids feel comfortable with what was going on, so I wanted to take them out bowling for the night.

Well, it wasn't!

When I got home with the kids a couple of hours later, I opened the front door and we found Darcy on the floor in a convulsion state. I told Michael to dial 911 immediately, but he was too upset, so I made a decision, instead of waiting for an ambulance, I decided to carry her to the backseat of the car.

We were about five minutes from the hospital so I knew I could get her there quickly.

Upon arriving at the Emergency Room, I yelled at Michael to watch Marissa, to be calm, and told him mom was going to be okay. I then went into the emergency room, and told the hospital staff she was a cancer patient of Dr. Greenberg and she had a treatment a few days ago, complaining about sores in her mouth. It was like they knew exactly what I was talking about.

Immediately, two staff nurses rush her into a room and I didn't know what was going on, but I knew it was bad because they started to yell those words again, the ones they used for Darcy's mom, Stat! Stat! Stat!

I started to realize that she might be dying, but then, I remembered those headlights that night and quickly said some prayers.

I then ran from the emergency area out to where the kids were. When I found them they were hysterical. I had to calm them both down saying over and over again, mommy is going to be alright, don't worry. After about five minutes, I finally calmed them both down.

I then had a talk with my son Michael. I told him your sister needs you right now, your mother needs you right now, and I need you right now. I know it's a lot to ask from you son, but I need you to step up and keep your sister calm. I grabbed him on both shoulders and gave him a hug saying it's going to be okay.

That was the night I saw my son become a young adult, ready for responsibility. He took control, was there for his sister, and he made me so proud!

I immediately got back to the nursing area where I saw Dr. Greenberg again, and I explain to her that we didn't eat steak. She asked what happened and I told her. Then she said, "Darcy was in a state of convulsion when you brought her in and now they're giving her IV fluids to bring her back. It was very serious Tony."

I told, Dr. Greenberg, "She wasn't drinking much all week, she complained of mouth sores, which I did make you aware of."

Then Dr. Greenberg said to me, "It was the combination of dehydration and the treatment Tony. She had very little fluid in her body, and we almost lost her tonight."

I was taken aback when I heard her say that. She then grabbed my shoulders and said, "Listen to me! I have treated a lot of people all my life, I want you to know I have never, ever seen a person with more strength, faith, courage, and resilience as your wife! Whatever faith she has, she has more than you can ever imagine. You are everything to her, and so are her children, and so is God. You both are going to beat this, but you have to make sure you communicate with each other so this doesn't happen again. I want you to go home now, there is nothing more you can do for her here, she's going to be okay in a few days."

As my kids and I walked out of the hospital that night my thoughts were, okay Lord, two chemo treatments down, two to go.

Chapter X
The Celebration

When Darcy got home a week later, after that horrific episode, we made sure we had talks about everything, even in front of the kids. We all talked about life, God, health, our family, and responsibility. We realized our kids were growing up quickly and it was amazing how resilient they were through all of what we've been through.

During this time, Michael focused more on his studies in school and was on his way to making the honor roll for a second straight semester. Marissa was doing great in school. She was now mainstreamed into regular classes, using her hearing aids. So school was going very well, and her playing basketball in the gym at night made it even better for her socially.

One night before Darcy's the third treatment, I decided to take a visit to the gym to watch Michael play and to say hi to everyone. The gym was packed like never before. When I walked through the gym door, I never expected what was going to happen next. I heard some group of people clapping in the far corner, and as I approached the inside, the applause got even louder.

As I went to see my scorekeepers, Dan and Cindy Gorman, all the people there started to stand, while yelling, cheering and screaming this name together "Tone..Simone! (clap, clap) Tone..Simone (clap, clap) Tone..Simone. I didn't know what was happening.

After a few minutes, when things calmed down, Dan and Cindy approached me and said, "You have been rewarded a new rap name by the kids. They all got together and planned this out. They had a feeling you were going to stop by tonight. It was a gift to you, from them that didn't cost much. Congratulations, your famous! You can thank your son's friends, Ben Cardilla and Jason Hinton for that, they came up with it. This means, when you do the TV show this year, you better make sure that you use that name to introduce yourself. They'll be expecting it."

I was completely surprised, humbled and didn't know what to say. But the love, thoughtfulness and feeling I received that night will never, *ever* be forgotten. Before I left, everyone in the gym that night made sure they asked me how Darcy was doing, and gave me big hugs of support.

Prior to Darcy's breast surgery with Dr. Adams, he recommend her to see a breast plastic surgeon for possible reconstruction, however she declined. Then one week before Darcy's next chemo treatment, she changed her mind and decided to see a plastic surgeon. This was another experience I'll never forget.

It was a little different, and on the borderline weird side. It was an appointment with a plastic surgeon to see if Darcy would like reconstruction. This was an interesting and disturbing appointment.

A doctor, whose name I can't even remember, calls us into his office and immediately says to me in a joking kind of voice, "Mr. Cimino, do you have a preference on how big you would like your wife's breasts to be?"

That took me aback and I said, "Excuse me Doctor?" He then started laughing.

Now Darcy was feeling pretty good this day and she kind of knew what to expect, so the joke really went over well with her. His next question was, "How are you both doing."

We said, fine doctor. He then said, with a chuckle, "Darcy, with your new breasts would you like nipples or no nipples?"

Now at this point, I started to get a little defensive to say the least, the doctor was not on good terms with me with all this joking he was doing. I stepped up and said, "Doctor, what exactly is this all about?"

He obviously understood my mood, and then he said, "Most men and women are a little nervous when they come into these consultations. I felt that spreading a little humor might make the atmosphere in the room a little less tense."

He must of sensed my thoughts because I kept quiet after that, I didn't like his humor. He then says, "Mr. Cimino listen, your wife was referred to me by Dr. Adams. He wanted you and Darcy to get a glimpse of what alternatives could be done to her body to enhance the area of her surgery, and I make that happen."

Angrily I told him, "I understand Doctor but I don't think this is a joking matter at all!"

"Okay, the next thing we're going to do is sit you both down at my desk while I bring out some albums with photos in them of actual women's breasts that I have performed reconstruction on."

We both said, okay and we decided to stay and listen.

What happens next would probably be a man's dream at a very strange buffet table, if you know what I mean. We saw pictures of every type of women's breasts you could possibly think of in these albums. He showed us pictures of what a women's breast would look like in sizes A, B's, and even Double D's. You name it, big, small, even petite. He then asks Darcy, "What do you prefer?"

Now, it was a time for a laugh, and at that time, laughs came at a premium price! After seeing about five hundred photos, it turned out I really wasn't a breast man after all. Darcy and I were both in agreement not to have this procedure done, so she decided to go with the other alternative, breasts prosthesis, which is an empty bra with two pockets sewn into a place where silicone gel like

84

implants are inserted manually. It was an easier way for her, and it avoided another surgery.

We left the doctor's office with multiple emotions. We got in the car, laughing, joking, crying. It was definitely an eye opening, unusual, entertaining experience. I then turned to Darcy jokingly saying, "We tell the kids everything right? Do you want to tell the kids about this appointment?"

"Definitely not!" she said laughing.

As the third chemotherapy treatment approached, we had a lot of conversation about everything that had happened so far and we were a little more careful about her diet, hydrating, resting, and not over exerting herself and it paid off.

Finally, a treatment that went smoothly. The only thing unusual that happened was I had to cut off a large clump of hair from Darcy's head due to all the chemotherapy, but it was expected and it went fine.

The following Sunday morning I got a pleasant surprise. The phone rang, and it turned out to be good ole' Mr. Plangere. He was calling me to see how Darcy was doing.

I told him we had a couple of rough moments, but the third treatment went really well. He said, "That's great Tony because I have some good news for you." He went on to say, "Every year for the past twenty years we have had an award called The Ernest W. Lass Public Service Award. As you know, Mr. Lass, was the owner of the newspaper some time ago and was always involved with community service. When his son, Donald Jr. heard about your volunteer work with the kids in your area and how you were also dealing with your wife's health, he immediately nominated you for this year's award."

After hearing that, I became speechless. Mr. P was asking if I was okay with receiving an award for my service, service that I do only out of the goodness of my heart, never looking for any kind of pat on the back or recognition. I couldn't thank him enough for this honor.

Mr. Plangere was very pleased and said, "Wonderful! We will see both of you at the ceremony. It will be on Monday, April fourteenth. Will you and Darcy be able to attend?"

"Wait Mr. P, let me look at the calendar to make sure Darcy's last treatment is finished." I checked the calendar and it was. I then told him providing everything goes to plan, and she's healthy, we would be honored to be there.

"Good, because we have something special there for her too."

I was so overwhelmed, I didn't know what to say. After many prayers at night, fabulous doctors, and a community of support like I never dreamed, Darcy made it through her fourth chemo treatment with flying colors.

The week before the ceremony, we got a call from Dr. Adam's office. Debbie, his office manager told me, "No worries Tony, Dr. Adams just wants to see both of you."

We went to visit Dr. Adams the week of April tenth, nineteen ninety-seven. We both get called into his office not knowing the conversation to come and we were both very nervous. As he sits us down at his desk, he says to us, "Hi guys, I have some great news for you. Congratulations Darcy, your other doctors and I have agreed and confirmed, you are cancer free!"

I cried out in a loud voice, "Oh my God!"

We both started crying, we couldn't believe what Dr. Adams just told us! It was something that Darcy's sisters Michele and Kathy never heard. She did it, she beat it! I said it over and over again, you did it, you did it, praise God up in Heaven, you beat it! What a moment it was for both of us! A moment we will never forget!

We immediately left the building to pick up Michael and Marissa from school. We brought them home and couldn't wait to tell them the great news. It was shear euphoria in our house that day.

Then my son, screams out something he's been wanting to say for a whole year, and that was, "Yay, we're going to Disney World!"

Grinning from ear to ear, and slapping him hi-five, I said, "Michael, you're right!"

At that moment, I got on the phone and started to make reservations for the Wilderness Lodge in Magic Kingdom, Walt Disney World, Florida.

My next call was to Mr. Plangere to let him know the great news. I said, "Mr. P, I have great news for you. Darcy was just told by her doctor today she's cancer free!"

"God bless both of you, that is great news Tony. So I guess we will see you and Darcy here on Monday in the atrium at ten a.m."

"We will be there Mr. Plangere. We are both excited about the event."

Over the weekend, I went back to work feeling good about everything that had happened, but humbled about it too, thinking about Darcy's sisters. I often thought about them over the course of the treatment. Darcy was always wondering, how and why cancer took her sister's lives at such a young age. I couldn't imagine how Darcy was feeling.

On the Monday morning of the awards ceremony, we both woke up at six a.m. and didn't know what to expect at the presentation. Prior to leaving home, I was advised to call the front desk .

When I called, the guard answered the phone and said, "Hello Mr. Cimino, I have been expecting your call, let me put you through to Mr. Plangere's secretary, Kathy."

Now, I knew Kathy just by going to Mr. P's office. She was always very nice and pleasant to me, but today she was extremely nice. She gave me instructions to drive up to the front of the building under the canopy where the entrance was, and a security guard, named Al, was going to come out and assist both of us into the building.

"Kath, Al doesn't have to do that."

"Tony, I am under specific instructions by Mr. Plangere to give you these directions."

"Okay Kathy. Thank you. See you soon."

We left home at nine forty-five in the morning. When we arrived at the front of the building around ten, there were quite a few cars parked in front already, but I did see Al in the distance.

When I approach him under the canopy, he directed me to a spot, had me roll down my window and said, "Tony, Darcy, good morning. I am here to take your keys so I can park your car."

"Al, I'm a pressman for Pete's sake, I can park my own car."

"Tony, I am under instructions to take your keys and park your car."

Then Darcy said to me while laughing, "Tony just give him your keys."

The next moment we had, was a moment we will never be able to consume, understand or appreciate enough. We got out of the car, approached the spinning doors that led us into the building, only to see hundreds and hundreds of people surrounding the rafters in the atrium around us, along with a standing room only mob down below.

As we walked in, everyone starts cheering and clapping to the highest levels I ever heard in that building. There were pressman I worked with on my shifts over the years there, people from the radio station they owned, office workers, some I knew, some I didn't. Electricians, news reporters, everyone that worked in the building. The applause was getting louder and louder. It was all for us!

There was an ambo in the middle of the atrium with a microphone. There was an American Cancer Society entourage there too. Mr. Plangere was there, Mr. Donald Lass, all the executives, all standing there clapping for Darcy and I. It was overwhelming! The applause lasted for about two minutes.

We didn't know how to react. They all knew what Darcy went through, they all knew about what our family went through, and they all wanted to show that no matter what, cancer could be beaten. They were there to voice it out.

I wondered then, how many of the people there cheering have lost loved ones like us, and maybe this was their time to show their pain and suffering in a great, positive way.

Then Mr. Plangere said, "What an inspiration you both are to everyone. While Darcy was going through cancer, Tony showed us what kind of person he is, and what kind of family he has. It gives me great pleasure to present the Ernest W. Lass Community Service award for Public Service to the highest degree to Tony Cimino!"

The applause was deafening.

As I went up to accept it, Mr. Donald Lass went to the microphone and said, "On behalf of the Asbury Park Press, and myself, I would like to present a check for one thousand dollars, in Darcy's name to the American Cancer Society. May we all see the day, cancer gets destroyed!"

Yes, April fourteenth, nineteen ninety-seven, a day that will go down in history for my family, the day our family really did beat cancer!

Chapter XI
Giving to God

For the next few months life was quiet for a change. Darcy's health was back to normal and we were able to get back to church on a more regular basis. Both Darcy and I were becoming more spiritual and more involved with the church too.

One Saturday mass, Father Gerard from Mt. Carmel Catholic Church, who often visited us at home when Darcy was sick, approached us about doing a couple of chores at church during and after mass.

Father Gerard asked Darcy if she would like to tend to the candle offerings and then he asked me if I would operate the new/old elevator that was put in the back of the church. This elevator was for handicapped parishioners who attended mass on weekends. Of course we both said yes.

My scheduled day to operate the elevator would be for Saturday afternoon mass at four p.m. Like I said though, it was an old/new elevator. You know the type of elevator that has a gate that you close after you get in, and a turnkey on the inside, to make it go up and down. Well, I said to Father Gerard, "Geez, Father Gerard, you couldn't get an elevator with push buttons? What if I get stuck in there?"

"No problem. Over here, you have an emergency phone and over there you have a push button bell. As far as the elevator, it cost ten grand, and we were lucky to get it."

Needless to say, I got stuck in it on the first day for an entire hour, and I ended up missing the whole four p.m. mass. However, I did get to know Rocco Giardelli a lot better, he was stuck in the elevator with me!

The following Saturday, Father Gerard approached me and said, "Tony, you need confession?"

"Excuse me, Father Gerard?"

"You missed mass last week, I thought you would want to come to confession."

"Excuse me Father Gerard, that stupid ten grand elevator you bought, well, I got stuck in it last week for over an hour!"

"Yes, I heard, but you also missed mass. I'll see you in confession later."

Tough priest that Father Gerard, but I loved him, he always went out of his way for our family. Whenever there was a sickness, or a problem at my job, or a marriage issue we needed to get resolved, he always made it very clear God had to be important in our lives.

Many of times we all fall into a trap of uncertainty not knowing what the next day will bring, in our case, it became the norm, with illness. Cancer struck us hard, but I have to say without the importance of faith in our life who knows how our lives would have turned out. We learned the power of prayer has an enormous strength to it.

I truly believe the more people who pray for you in moments of your own despair, God hears those prayers being called, and then with his power, miracles do occur in those sudden crucial moments of our lives. I found this out early on in my own life, it was undeniable that God strengthened my heart and my mind during critical times growing up. A grand-mom dying in front of me, getting robbed at knife point, my mom dying after I got married. The one most important thing I learned early on in my life was how precious life really is.

For some reason, I was given this gift of strength to overcome these tragedies and obstacles and learned to care for people even more, while tending to my own family. I knew these events in my life were going to shape what kind of person I was going to be, and I also knew I had to give back to people what I have learned.

In learning this, I made sure first to give back to God, whether it be a chore at church, helping someone in need, or just being there for a friend or family member who needed me. Whatever the case, I made sure God was going to be a mainstay of importance in our families lives forever.

Chapter XII
A Humbling Journey

After that elevator incident, the following Monday, I showed up at work and a bunch of guys come up to me saying, did you hear what happened?

"No I didn't hear anything, what's up."

They said, your buddy Mr. Plangere sold the newspaper for three hundred million dollars. I was taken aback by the news, my first thought like everyone else was, do we still have a job? Then my next thought was sadness because of the relationship I had with him.

The first chance I was able to get, I wanted to go talk to him about it.

The following day, I knocked on his door, and he said, "Tony, come on in. I'm sure you heard by now."

I said in a joking voice, "Yes, you're selling the paper and you didn't tell me!"

He knew many employees were upset, after all, the company was a family owned business for over one hundred thirty years and people and employees didn't expect anything like this to happen.

He asked me how I felt about it. I told him I was very sad, worried, and I know the guys in the pressroom were too. But, I understood. I told him, it's your business, your company that your family built, and ever since this computer came out I could see where the newspaper was going.

Mr. Plangere then said to me, "I want you to know something, and I want this kept between the two us. Tony, I appreciate all my employees, they are the backbone of this company, however I cannot guarantee what is going to happen when the new company comes in, but I want you to know, I will never forget my employees and I would never disrespect them in any way, and that's all I'm going to say to you about that."

He went on to say, "Your job is to take care of that beautiful wife of yours and your family. For as long as I've known you Tony, you don't have anything to worry about, you just keep doing what you're doing. With everything you and your family have been through, I have no doubts about your success."

He then shook my hand for the last time and I gave him a hug. I walked out of his office with a sadness in my heart.

On the first day of acquisition, we were all called out to that same atrium in the front entrance where I accepted the Ernest W. Lass Community Service Award. There were about five hundred people in there again, only difference was, you could hear a pin drop this time. It was very disturbing because we knew this was a corporate meeting, not a family meeting, especially when Mr. P. was absent from the event.

Then this man steps up to the microphone and welcomes everyone to the new Gannett USA Today newspaper. He said, "Hello everyone, I am your new boss and publisher and my name is Robert Crawford."

I don't know why, but at that moment, I got an eerie feeling about him, because it looked like he was looking directly at me, but then again, I may have been a little paranoid.

He then went on to say the professional mumbo jumbo we're all so used to hearing at corporate events. Then all of a sudden, the next words that came out of his mouth caught everyone by surprise.

"As you know we are a big new company. And if there is not a position for you here, there will be open transfers for you at any one of our other locations. Anytime you wish to leave, my door is always open and I will try to accommodate your desires on where you would like to relocate to. We have many newspapers all over the United States, and anytime your services are needed at any one of these locations, that's where you'll be heading."

After that statement, I along with everyone around me, had the same sentiments. Who, where and when are we leaving!

The meeting lasted another hour after that with corporate officers speaking about the process and our new 401k package and benefits.

Mostly a negative feeling throughout the building was felt from the newsroom to the plate room, thru the circulation department down to the pressroom. Lots of discussions about relocation and where we're heading over the next few years, and no one felt safe with their job.

While all this was going on, I received a phone call from my brother Tom, you know, the one who used to work at the racetrack selling green handicapper sheets at the kiosk. He said to me, "Tony, I just received some bad news, is there any way you can get down to Florida anytime soon?"

Tom had been living there for the last twenty years, since our mom died. I said, "Tom, Mr. Plangere just sold the newspaper to a new company, I don't think it would be a good idea for me to leave right now, how about in a couple of months?"

"Tony, I'm dying of the same cancer mom had, I have Hodgkin's Lymphoma."

I couldn't believe what I just heard. I thought not again. I then said, "Tom, how long have you had it?"

"About six months or so. The doctors said I have about two years to live, if I'm lucky."

Hearing this news, I felt a responsibility, a family obligation and love for my brother to get to Florida immediately to see him. With Darcy's approval of course, I went to visit my brother often over the next six months and visit with some of his doctors too.

There was no good news on the forefront, no cure, just radiation and chemotherapy treatments to prolong the cancer.

At this point in my life, I started to get worn down, tired of hearing, dealing and watching cancer tear up my family. So I called upon my faith once again to get me through this, and to be strong for my brother.

I was feeling depressed about all the extracurricular activities in my life. Activities I was so excited about doing as a hobby, started to turn into more of a job and a responsibility. From the Board of Education, Directing Recreation activities and possibly making a run at Mayor in my town, it didn't seem to matter anymore. My focus became my brother and fortunately at the time my own family was doing great. That made coping with my brother a lot easier. Darcy's cancer was in remission, Marissa was playing basketball and Michael was in school earning Honors in science, math and lettering in bowling.

As the months were going by, more and more, I was asking the new company (Gannett) for time off to visit, and tend to my brother. It was starting to get very trying on my wife. I would leave without notice and she would take care of home and the kids.

Sometimes I would leave for two or three days to make sure my brother was getting the necessary chemotherapy treatment for the week. I can remember one doctor visit, he had to have bone marrow taken out of his hip, it had to be one of the most excruciating procedures I have ever seen.

I kept thinking about everyone in the family who dealt with cancer, and how Darcy was the only one to survive it. I was thinking about my mom's death, and remembering how much pain she went through with this

Hodgkin's disease, and wondering how and when my brother was going to die from it.

After another visit to my brother in Tampa, I came back home once again. I remember feeling completely depressed that I had go to work on a day I just didn't feel like going.

When I got there I asked my boss/foreman on the floor, Al Truax, if it was okay just to clean the presses for the day. It's a very inky, dirty job to say the least, but my head and focus was not into doing million dollar sales color advertisement jobs on the paper that day. So I asked Al if he could give me a pass. Al knew what was happening with my brother. He told me, sure it's good with me, go ahead and clean units/machines four and five.

As the presses started up, I was cleaning the shut down press machines as required. Then about a half hour later, I started feeling a pain in my stomach, sort of like a gut wrenching pain, like I was supposed to be with my brother that day. I can remember being on my knees profusely crying inside the machine I was working in. It was a good place for me to be at the time because the presses were so loud, no one could see or hear me.

But then my boss Al showed up. Immediately, I tried to compose myself, he then picked me up off the floor from inside the machine, grabbed me by the arm, dragged me out and said, go clean up, we need to talk.

I started thinking I was going to get fired for all the time I missed. Instead, he brought me into his office, sat me down and said, "Tony, the corporate brass was having discussions about you and they decided it would be best for you to be with your brother at this time. They thought it would be a good idea for you to consider a permanent transfer down to Ft. Myers, Florida. It's sunny, warm and the Fort Meyers Newspaper Press is only an hour away from your brother."

I was thinking, if this was Mr. Plangere's idea, I would run with it, but my thoughts were saying, wait a minute, I remember how this new company came in and said there would be a transfer available for people who were interested. Only problem was, I wasn't really interested in one, but my brother really needed me there and I figured this was a calling to do that.

The following Monday before my shift, I received a phone call at home from Mr. Crawford's secretary, who happened to be Mr. Plangere's old secretary. Kathy asked me, "Tony, Mr. Crawford would like to meet with both you and your wife tomorrow afternoon around two o'clock, are you both available?"

I told her we would both be there.

The next day Darcy and I go to the front entrance, and Al, the security guard was no longer there. A new security guard, named Pete, escorted us to Mr. Crawford's room in the upstairs atrium office. A beautiful office with a view which happened to be Mr. Plangere's old office. It definitely did not have the same warmth as it had before.

Mr. Crawford, President and Publisher invites us in, and welcomes both of us in a very warm way. Shaking my hand, at first glance he looked like Donald Trump with black hair, then hugging Darcy, he said it's such a pleasure to meet both of you. I heard the story about you two and I find it most inspirational and rewarding. He was also saying what a model employee I was and how the new staff from Gannett was looking forward to having a long lasting, favorable relationship with me. He heard about my awards and the relationship I had with Mr. Plangere. For the first few minutes, I was thinking, maybe this guy was okay and the meeting was going to be a good one. I was wondering why he called me in first place.

Then the sales pitch came. He said, "Tony," in an intimidating type of voice. "How would you like to be transferred and head up our Ft. Myers Pressroom? We seem to be having some union/employee problems down there and hearing how many times you have visited your brother this past year in Tampa, maybe this might be a good fit for you and Darcy." He then motioned to us, "Follow me for a minute, I want you both to come with me."

He brought us out to his secretary, Kathy, and said to her, "Kathy, is the package ready, and in order for Darcy and Tony?"

With a smile, Kathy answered, "Yes Mr. Crawford, here it is."

Then we follow Mr. Crawford into a different office.

We both are thinking, what the hell is going on.

They bring us into this room with a large corporate type rectangle desk, sit us down and start to explain our moving/transfer conditions.

I immediately say, "Excuse me Mr. Crawford, what exactly are you getting at?"

"Tony, here you go, we have some golf shirts for you with your name and the Gannett logo on it, pens for you Darcy, and this binder right here is a layout and itinerary for all your moving expenses from travel, food and beverage services including hotel/Condo accommodations until you find a home."

Stunned and taken aback, I put my hands up and said, "Wait, Mr. Crawford, as much as I appreciate the offer and what you are offering, I need at least a couple of weeks to discuss this situation with Darcy. I have to sell my house, move my kids out of school, and move from a place I have been living all of my life. There's a lot to think about here!"

"Nonsense Tony! You're the guy we want down there, we've made all the arrangements, all the phone calls to the proper people, negotiated your salary transfer with a hefty bonus and a nice raise, and put this moving expense package through for an easy transition."

"Mr. Crawford, with all due respect, can you at least give me a day to think about it?"

"Absolutely, go home, talk with Darcy, and get things in order. However, be prepared to leave next week."

"Mr. Crawford, next week is kind of sudden isn't it? To move my job, my wife, my kids, my community work, my parish and my life in New Jersey for forty years all in one week?"

And then, it ALL came out, why we had this meeting in the first place.

Mr. Crawford said, "Tony, I have made you an adequate and generous offer correct? Listen to what I am going to say to you. I chose you to be transferred for a number of reasons, one was because of your brother, second you are a role model employee of this company, and one of the best we have. Finally, you have a track record of community involvement like no one else. You know people, you know how they think, act and talk. I need you to go down there to represent yourself as a company man. We have a union dispute going on there between the Ft. Myers pressman and the USA Today newspaper pressman, and we need everyone on the same page so we don't have a strike. And you're the one we're going to send down there to fill in a new pressman position. It's a lateral move for you, but most of all a strategic move for us."

I then asked the ultimate question to Mr. Crawford. "If I fail to accept this offer, will I still have my job here?"

With a sinister kind of smirk, Mr. Crawford looked at me and said, "Let's put it this way, you're never going to get a better offer than what I just gave you, as a matter of fact, we think it would be in your best interest to accept this offer, not only for you but for your brother and your family."

I looked at Darcy and I knew exactly what she was thinking. We both thought we had no choice, so I took the offer and headed down to Ft. Meyers the following week. However, before I left, I made sure the whole family knew what was going on.

My kids were not happy, they had to leave their school that was so important to them. We had to put our house up for a quick sale, and I approached community council in my town and advised them of our move. Our friends were upset, wondering why we were making such a rash decision. They thought it had something to do with my brother's illness, so I left it at that.

My last and most important stop before I left was a visit to Our Lady of Mt. Carmel Church to say goodbye to Father Gerard. After all, I was baptized there, went to school there, we were married there, and our children were baptized there. That had to be the toughest place to leave behind.

Father Gerard wished us well, gave us a blessing and said, "Don't worry about anything, where you both go, God will be there for you always. Good luck and always remember to come here if you ever come back to visit." We hugged each other and we felt that leaving that church was a loss we would never be able to replace.

That night, my friends organized a party at a pub called Pats Tavern. About fifty people showed up.

They had a plan in mind and they were going to make sure it was a good party. I mean after all, I was with some of them for over twenty years, and most of my friends who were there, I knew for about for forty years. Policeman that I knew so well, fireman, who never get enough credit for what they do, councilman, pressman I worked with for over twenty years, you name it, they all showed up.

First thing on their agenda that night was a toast. My friend, post office cleaner and fellow pressman, Gene was the first one to speak. "Everyone, let's all put our straws in this vodka cocktail bowl. Then after my toast, everyone must tell a little story about how you know Tony. After each toast, we all take a sip out of the vodka bowl at the same time."

Sounded great to me, I'm thinking, should be fun hearing all these stories. Only problem though, I found out later, the joke was on me!

Turned out, everyone was fake drinking the vodka while yours truly was the only one consuming it! I had a feeling something was up, just didn't figure it out at the time. So, I just went with it. I said to myself, no worries, why not, I'm never going to see these guys again and I might as well enjoy the night.

The party lasted several hours. It was like I never wanted it to end, because I knew where I was going, and who I was leaving behind. Depression definitely played a part on this night. So their plan worked. They got me drunk, brought me home, and playfully dropped me off on the front lawn to think about what I was going to miss when I left. It was a great party.

Only thing though, Darcy was not in a very playful mood that night, to say the least. Especially after seeing me on our front lawn in the condition I was in. It didn't really matter that night how many years I was happily married. Understandably so, I couldn't walk straight!

When I got to the front door the first of two pillows thrown from the top of the stairs knocked me off my feet. She wasn't a happy camper because I was leaving for Fort Myers in the morning.

Thinking back on that whole night, it should have been a sign for what was going to come next.

I woke up the next day, packed up the car in the morning, hangover and all, while Darcy was kind enough to make me a cup of coffee before I left. My itinerary had me driving down to Lorton, Virginia to catch the Amtrak auto train. Then, a sixteen hour train ride down to Sanford, Florida.

When I arrived, I had to wait to get my car off the train. After getting the car, I then headed south for the Ft. Myers News Press.

I arrived there around four in the afternoon. I was greeted by the Human Resources Director, John Perkins. He then escorts me inside to his office, offers me a cup of coffee and says, before we get started I need to advise some people that you just arrived.

About fifteen minutes later, he shows up with the Pressroom Manager, the lead pressman of all the crews and the Head Pressroom Foreman, to discuss my working environments and conditions of my job.

We all sit down and exchange pleasantries and Mr. Perkins then said, "I hear you have been briefed about what is going on down here with our labor union conditions."

"Yes sir, I am aware of them."

"I want you to know, under no circumstance should you feel threatened or intimidated about working here."

My immediate response was, "Why should I feel threatened or intimidated?" What had me worried was the next response by the Pressroom Manager. It was something I felt I really needed to be concerned about.

The Pressroom Manger Pete then said, "Your fellow pressman on all shifts are aware of your arrival Tony, and were chirping about the new guy coming down from Jersey."

Not understanding, I asked, "Why?"

"Well," continued Pete. "I think there is some jealousy going on around here because they heard about the arrangements and package deal you received to come here. Not many pressman have come here from as far as Jersey. So they're a little suspicious about your being here."

I then said, "My reason for being here is to work and that's it."

Pete coyly said, "Then there shouldn't be a problem, everything should go smoothly."

I felt somewhat rushed after that remark, like the conversation needed no longer to proceed, and figured it was time to leave. Then after they said thank you and good luck, the meeting ended and I headed to my temporary residence, which was a condominium on the south side of Fort Myers which was part of my relocation package. I was able to stay there until I found a home for my family.

When I finally arrived there, I immediately called Darcy and told her about my arrival and my meeting. While she was listening she interrupted me and started asking me about my safety. I couldn't agreed with her more as I was feeling kind of anxious and nervous, but I figured it was just job jitters. I then said to her, "Listen honey, I'm here, I might as well get used to things, start looking at houses, schools and areas to familiarize myself with, and most importantly, a Catholic Church."

I had about a week before I started work, so it was my job as a husband, and a dad, to get things ready for the family to move.

After about a week, I was fortunate enough to find a beautiful three bedroom, two bath house with a pool and a garage in a fantastic area for ninety-nine thousand dollars. It seemed like it was a great house for the money and it was in a great area with schools and Catholic church close by.

I started thinking maybe I was just jumping to conclusions and feeling paranoid about work. Finding that beautiful home, great schools and Catholic church for my family made me feel secure enough to put ten thousand dollars down on the house and we were on our way!

That night, I called Darcy and told her about the house I found for us. She said you're not going to believe this Tony, but a wonderful couple interested in our house just signed the contract and put the same amount of money down. We thought this was great news. Even Michael and Marissa started to get used to the idea of moving. Darcy had a great way of selling Disney World to them, and how we would be season ticket holders when we moved there. So even they were starting to get a little excited about the move.

When I got off the phone with Darcy, I immediately called my brother Tom, and told him the news of moving and he was very excited about having me close by.

That Sunday, the day before my first day at my new job I went to church. Did you ever hear the saying when you pray "prayers are for us to say in our time, but the prayers we say are answered in God's time?" Well, on my first day at work, I realized after my shift was over that night, my prayers would be answered in God's time, not in my time.

I arrived at work fifteen minutes early. You know the other line, in one of those famous movies, "if you're five minutes early you're on time, if you're on time your late," well I had no problem with that. I wanted to show the new employees I was committed to the job as soon as possible, and I wanted to make a good first impression.

After that, I went to the break room as always to get a cup of coffee, like all pressman do before they go to work. It was in that break room, fifteen minutes later, when the first incident occurs with my new fellow co-workers.

There were seven pressman in that break room that night. I poured my first cup of coffee and as I was putting my sugar and cream in, I looked up and they were gone. I said to myself, if this is how it's going to be, fine, union or no union, I have a job to do.

I get to the floor and the first thing I look for in the pressroom is the position sheet. The position sheet tells each pressman which press line he is on and where he is working for the night, such as paper handler (loading rolls of white newsprint to feed into the machines from downstairs), or press lead (setting color on the newspaper upstairs). The head foreman puts the position sheet out every night to let you know your assignment for that work day.

Only problem was, my name was not on the sheet on either sides of the pressroom. The Ft. Meyers Press non-union side nor the USA Today union side.

In my mind now I'm thinking, is this some sort of sabotage or is it just an honest mistake. I immediately visit the pressroom manager's office to see why this happened. After all, none of the pressman were going to explain it to me. Heck, they wouldn't even have a cup of coffee with me.

The answer I received from the pressroom manager was, I forgot. I then said, okay, where do you want me to work? He asked me if I was a union man or a company man. I replied in an angry voice, "What? A company man of course."

He then told me to work on the Ft. Myers side downstairs in the pressroom and take out the waste paper trash all night until the end of the shift. I had to record the weight after each dump and report it to him after the shift was over.

From that moment on, I knew there was going to be trouble. I knew this because a twenty year experienced pressman usually is not stationed downstairs in the bowels of the pressroom to take waste paper dumps out. It's normally for an inexperienced, untrained pressman. My feeling was not to cause a commotion at this time because I was the new guy on the block, so to speak. So, for the next few hours, I was just concentrating on my job which wasn't very hard because it was one of those jobs I used to do when I first started.

Finally, halfway through the shift a conversational breakthrough occurred.

A black man about fifty years old named Jesse approached me. I say a black man in a non prejudicial way because he was the only black male working there at the time and the only person that talked to me.

Jesse said to me, "Tony I hear you're from New York."

"No, actually New Jersey."

"Well, I'm from Brooklyn."

Happy to have some conversation with a fellow employee, I smiled and said, "My dad and grand-pop were from Brooklyn."

"I'm glad you said that, you see those red-necks over there to the left?" asked Jesse.

Turning to look, I said, "Yeah."

He then motioned to the other side and said, "You see those guys over there to the right?"

"Yeah." I was wondering where Jesse was going with this.

Finally, Jesse said in a very quiet voice, "I'm going to tell you something now, and you didn't hear it from me. If you say anything about it, I will deny it."

Feeling myself getting angry, I replied, "Okay Jesse, I won't say anything."

In a quiet tone, Jesse proceeded to say, "I heard about your transfer and I know you're a good man, I heard about all those things you have done for kids up there and other folks. These folks down here are a little different, they have a way about them. You see, they don't like too many folks."

At this point, Jesse grabs my arm and puts it next to his and continues, "Your Italian right?"

"Yeah."

"We're pretty close, they're not, you get what I'm saying?"

"I think so."

"Tony, they're out to get you son, every last one of them, they don't want you here, they don't like you, they say you're trouble."

Hearing this really upset me. "Jesse I'm not trouble!"

"Son, I know that. But there's a union riff going on here and you were put here for a reason, so watch your back. That's the last thing I'm going to say to you, figure it out."

I walked away from that conversation nervous, scared and unsure about how to take his words to me. I knew the man went out of his way to inform me, and protect me and I felt very grateful about that.

I then continued my night without any other occurrences, finished my job, and gave my figures to the boss as requested.

I left for home scared out of my wits end. It was about four in the morning when I got home that night, so I couldn't call Darcy to tell her what happened, so I went straight to bed.

I woke up the next morning at ten, thinking what am I going to do now. I figured maybe I should have a backup plan.

I went to Dunkin Donuts, bought a newspaper, of all things a Fort Myers Press and I immediately started looking for jobs. Only problem was, most of them down in Florida paid half the salary of what I was earning, so it was going to be a tall task to find something comparable. I called an automobile dealer in the area and low and behold they set me up for an interview.

The name of the dealership was Fort Myers Ford. They were looking for sales people at the time and they liked my personality and resume enough to offer me a position on the floor selling cars for four hundred dollars a week. It was about half of what I was earning at the newspaper but I figured you never know, better to have a job lined up.

I didn't want to tell Darcy about it just yet, I wanted to make sure I wasn't jumping to conclusions. However, I did call her disguising my concerns, just to let her know everything is going to be okay down here. I then went to dinner, and then to my second day at the new job.

I arrived early as usual and immediately the same treatment happened again. I enter the break room for my coffee, and everyone immediately walks out. I then go to look for the position sheet to see where I work and my name is left off of it again.

After that, there was a confrontation between me and three pressman outside the break room. They surround me and question me, "Who's side are you on?"

"Excuse me? I'm here to do a job, that's it guys."

Another pressman then said, "I hear you're a union buster."

Getting disgusted, I told him, "You heard wrong pal."

A third pressman chimed in, "If you want to continue to work here you better start making friends in a hurry."

After that, they all laughed and walked away.

I immediately went to the pressroom manager's office and explained to him what had just happened. His reply was, you got the same job as last night, just get me the figures when you're done. That was it, and he walked away.

I didn't know how to handle any of this, all I could do was go downstairs and do my job. I had a family to worry about. It wasn't like I could just walk away and quit.

I then approached Jesse. He gave me a look, shook his head at me and walked away. I knew at that point this was going to be a problem. I just didn't know how long it would last.

When my shift was over, I handed in my figures, went into the locker room, got dressed, and not one person in there said anything to me, not even as I walked out the door to go home.

I went to my car, and started to head home. As I was leaving the parking lot I turned left on the main road and realized there was a car from my job, following right behind me. They had their head lights turned off.

I turned around to get a look at them, and as soon as I did that, the driver put his high beams on to blind me and then started to tailgate me.

The faster I drove, the faster he sped up. The more evasive maneuvers I did, the more he stayed with me.

Finally, in the distance, I saw a police car parked on the side of the road and I started to flash my lights on and off to get their attention. When I did that, the car that was following me the whole time shut his lights off and made the first turn out of sight.

Approaching the police car, I stopped immediately to inform him of my situation. The police officer asked me, "Did you get the plate number from the car that was tailgating you? A color, or a look at the driver?"

"No officer, his high beams were on and I couldn't see a thing."

He then asked where I was coming from at four o'clock in the morning. I told him work. He suggested, "Maybe you might want to have a talk with your Human Resources department tomorrow and see what they could do for you. As for me, I can only write down a report based on what you told me. You really have no evidence to support your claim, but if I were you, first thing in the morning, I would visit your Human Resources department. and advise them what happened."

I thanked him for his help and advice. He then asked me, "By the way, where are you from?"

"Jersey."

"I figured, sounded like it, I'm from New York myself. You better be careful down here pal, the gun laws are different, people are different, it's not the north, you can carry a gun."

"I'm learning as I go officer, thank you again, have a good night."

The next morning, which was Wednesday, I took the officer's advice, got dressed and decided to head down to the Human Resources department. However, before I left the condo, I got an unexpected telephone call from Ft. Myers Ford. It was the General Manager. "Tony, this is Jimmy Smith. We reviewed your resume and would like to offer you a position with our dealership."

I told Jim, "I am very grateful for the opportunity and I appreciate the offer, but would you mind if I gave you an answer in about a week?"

"No problem. We would be glad to have you on our team!"

"Thank you Jim, I will let you know either way by next week."

I figured it was time to call Darcy. I was threatened last night, so this was no time to fool around and not tell her the truth. I called and her immediately response was for me to go to personnel. Her exact words were "Right now!" I told her I was on my way. She then asked, What are we supposed to do about our house? What about the kids, school, the down payment on the house down there? She was frantic on the phone.

I told her, "Honey listen, we both lost our moms, you lost both of your sisters, you beat cancer, my brother's dying, hear me out on this. I have a backup plan, it's contingent on how personnel is going to handle this situation. An automobile dealership offered me a job starting at four hundred dollars a week, plus a car to drive. I can start tomorrow. If we decide that's not an option, that's fine too. Right now we'll just take it one step at a time, it will all work out. God has always given us the strength to persevere and He will help get us through this situation as well. Remember, the headlights the night before your surgery? Well, funny thing isn't it, I had headlights on me last night, only in a different way. Everything will be okay."

She calmed down, and said, "I love you, call me after the meeting, as soon as it is over!"

I said, "I love you too, and I will the first chance I get."

When I got to the Ft. Myers News Press building, I made sure no one saw me walk in because who knows the repercussions it could have if anyone I worked with recognized me there.

I approached the front desk and asked for the Human Resources Manager, Mr. Perkins. The secretary told me he was in a meeting and she didn't know how long he would be. I then said, "Fine, my name is Tony Cimino. I was recently transferred here from New Jersey."

She said, "I heard about you."

"Good, because I need to speak to Mr. Perkins immediately, I was threatened last night going home after work, and this could be a matter of life and death."

Looking concerned, she immediately called him and within ten minutes I was in his office.

I walked in and said, "Mr. Perkins, my name is Tony Cimino."

"Yes, I remember you," replied Mr. Perkins.

"Good. Have you been aware of any incidents going on in the pressroom lately?"

Confused, he told me, "No, please explain what you mean."

I proceeded to tell him everything I have been through. The coffee room incident, the pressman Jesse warning me about possible confrontations with other pressman, my name not being on the work sheet, and then advising the Pressroom Manager about the incidents, who totally ignored the situation.

And the topper, leaving work last night, a car with its high beams on tailgating me all the way home in a destructive, threatening, manner until fortunately, I approached a police car and they finally sped off. He could not believe what he was hearing.

Then I explained to him why I was transferred here in the first place. I told him my brother was ill and that Mr. Crawford offered me a transfer package to accommodate me so I could be there for my brother during his illness. The other factor was to implement me here to represent the company in a union work environment. Mr. Crawford said this would be a lateral move that would benefit both of our concerns. I then accepted his offer and was assumed it would be a smooth transition. Unfortunately, that hasn't been the case. I already bought a house here and presently my house is sold back in New Jersey.

Mr. Perkins then looks at me sternly and said, "Tony, I want you to stay right here and do not leave this office."

I was sitting in his office for about a half an hour, when finally he returns with the Vice President in charge of

Operations, the Editor of the Newsroom and the Editor's secretary to take down notes.

Mr. Perkins then says, "Gentlemen, we are going to conference call Mike Lorenco, the Human Resources Director up in Jersey. We're going to discuss our options and solutions to this problem."

Totally frustrated and angry I told them, "You guys need to figure out this mess!"

Mr. Perkins proceeded to call Mr. Lorenco, and explained everything to him. Mike, after hearing the news, is speechless. Mr. Perkins asks Mike, "Are you still with us? What are you thinking?"

Mike answered in an angry voice, "Tony, where are you staying?"

"The condo you guys put me in, on the south side of town."

Mike then said, "Well I think the first thing we should do is get you out of there." Everyone was in agreement with that idea.

"The second thing we need to know is, who is involved, can you identify them?"

"Yes, but I don't want to jeopardize my life by you guys going out there and telling anyone what's going on!"

Mike said, "Absolutely not. We wouldn't do that."

Mike then asks Mr. Perkins, "Is there a high rise hotel in the area, away from the newspaper?"

Mr. Perkins said, "Yes, the Marriot on the north side of town, near the river."

"Fine, let's put Tony up there in the penthouse suite until we find out how we're going to handle this situation."

They all agreed. Then Mike said, "Tony, do you have your car?"

"Yes Mike, I brought it down here on auto train."

"Okay," said Mike. "Here's what you're going to do. Someone there is going to escort you to your car and to that

114

hotel. You are to stay there until you hear from me, understood? You don't even go out of that hotel to eat. You eat there. We will pick up all the expenses, don't worry about what's happening. I'm going to give you my personal home phone and my secretary's home phone. I want you to call us anytime you feel the need to call, about anything, do you understand?"

"I understand Mike, but can you tell me one thing."

"What's that Tony?"

"Am I going to have a job after this?"

"Of course you are."

I then asked, "Is it going to be here?"

Furiously Mike replied, "Hell no, we're going to bring you back home. I just need some time to figure out the logistics to make that happen."

Finally Mr. Perkins speaks up and says, "How do you want us to spin this Mike?"

Mike told him, "Put a gag order on it. Not a word about it. We're bringing him back here. I'll be in touch with you later on today."

Then Mike hung up, and Mr. Perkins asked me, "Can you make a positive ID of everyone who threatened you Tony?"

"Everyone except the guys in the car last night."

Next, Mr. Perkins asked his secretary to get a name and photo listing of all the pressroom employees.

She returns to the office and then asks me, "Tony can you identify all who were involved?"

I proceeded to indentify all those involved. When finished, she asked me if I needed anything. I sarcastically said, "Yeah, can you get me a house? I got a couple tied up right now that I really can't call home anymore."

She said, "Don't worry, it will all get worked out. For now, let's get you over to that Marriot."

She then called a newspaper reporter, Joe, and gave him instructions to follow me to my condo. Once there, I had to get my belongings together and follow him over to the Marriot across town.

It was a beautiful hotel on the river. Once in, I went to the front desk and the concierge took over from there. He took my luggage, brought me up to the room and asked me if I wanted something to eat or drink. I said, not unless you get one for yourself. He started to laugh and said, "Dinner reservations have been made for you, I was specifically given instructions that you eat in your room, it has a beautiful view. Is that ok?"

"Yup, great, thanks."

I called Darcy, who was frantic waiting to hear from me. I told her about the meeting and how they escorted me to a high rise hotel, how I had to identify all involved and I had strict instructions not to even leave my hotel room. Darcy was in tears, and so upset that I was there alone going through all of this. I reassured her everything was in God's hands and we were going to be okay. Underneath it all, I was very worried and concerned, but I made sure not to convey any of that to her.

Darcy then said, "Well, I have some more bad news for you." I thought to myself what now! She continued, "I had a talk with the realtor about our situation and what was happening down there with you, but the buyers on our house insist they will not back out of the contract. They said they are sorry, but they love our house, and they will sue us if we make any attempt to back out of the contract."

"It's okay. We'll just take one step at a time. Did you tell the kids about what was going on?"

"I told Michael. He wants to come down there and beat those guys up!"

"I figured, he's thirteen years old, what's he supposed to think, hell," I said jokingly, "I want to beat

116

them up too! You should see the room I'm in. Twenty-fifth floor, penthouse, beautiful view of the river. We will have to visit someday."

"Huh," she said. "What! You think I'll ever visit that place after what they have done to you and our family!"

"Honey, I'm just kidding, it will be okay."

I now hear a beep on the phone, indicating a call coming in so I hang up with Darcy. It's about six o'clock, just before dinner. The phone call is from Mike Lorenco from the Asbury Park Press. He asked me if I'm alright and if my accommodations are satisfactory. I told him as far as the hotel, it's great, as far as my life right now and my family, not so great. Mike told me not to worry, we have a plan to get you back here.

Mike told me, "Here is the plan. You have your old position back, you are no longer employed by the Ft. Myers newspaper, and you will receive no further calls from them. They are completely out of the picture. If you receive a call from them, you are to hang up and call me immediately. I don't think that will happen, but it's better to be cautious with this situation we're dealing with right now."

Mike continued, "On Friday morning, early, about three in the morning, you are to get in your car, and drive directly to Sanford, Florida auto train. You have a ten a.m. train reservation. When you arrive, they will check you in, load your car on the train and you are to board for a four p.m. departure. It's about a four to five hour drive from Ft. Myers, that will give you enough time to have breakfast before you arrive there. Oh, one other thing, I also reserved a sleeper car for you. As far as the costs, everything is paid for and taken care of by us. We just want you to take your time, be careful driving, and by no means are you to go out of that hotel tomorrow, at all. Do you understand everything?"

"Yes Mike, thank you for your help."

"We are doing this because of a recent death threat that has been made to your life. That is why you are in that hotel, so please, no calls other than your wife, not even any friends at this time, not until you get on that train."

Hearing those actual words coming from Mike's mouth really left me feeling scared and feeling kind of numb. I then told Mike, "Thanks for everything and for being there for me."

"No worries pal, you're a good man, you certainly did not deserve this. I'll see you first thing Monday morning."

I then called Darcy back and told her the plans and itinerary Mike Lorenco made for my return home. The only thing I did not tell her at that time was about the death threat. I could hear the relief in her voice as she said, "Thank God, I love you, I'll see you Saturday when you get home."

Finally after a long two weeks of stress, I arrived home Saturday afternoon. Darcy greeted me at the door with the kids. They were relieved I was home and amongst the hugs and kisses, I was getting bombarded with questions about where we're going to live. I said, guys relax, I called the realtor, we have an appointment tomorrow. She found a nice three bedroom one bath home two miles from here, it's going to be okay.

My son, Michael, then says, "Dad, does this really mean were moving from this house?"

"Son, sometimes in life you can't control things that happen, you can only go with the flow to make life easier, and right now, we are forced to sell this house we have lived in for almost ten years. The wrong doing that's been done, maybe someday we will have an answer for it, but as for now, I'm home safe, we're all okay and you should know, mom and I will always find a great way to make things work out."

The next day, the realtor brought us over to what would become our new home. We all decided this is the neighborhood in Neptune City we wanted to live in. It was called Ridge Place. It was a nice small community and had many people we knew who lived there, so it was a perfect fit!

We moved into our new house and the press gave me a week off to get situated.

On Monday, I returned to my pressroom position. First on the agenda, I had a meeting with Mike Lorenco, the Human Resources director who guided me back here, along with Mr. Crawford who sent me down to Florida in the first place. At the meeting, I met a former Human Resources Director, who was recently transferred and promoted to editor.

The meeting started out by Mr. Crawford saying, "So what exactly happened after you left here Tony?"

As if I had to explain to him again what I went through, I said, "Mr. Crawford, weren't you briefed on the situation?"

"Yes, but I want to hear it from you."

"You put me into the middle of a union labor dispute environment between union employees and company workers. Why did you do that? I almost got killed down there!"

Mr. Crawford rose from his seat, looked me in the eye, and firmly said, "The situation called for a role model employee and you were the one we decided to send, besides we thought it would be a good fit knowing you missed some time at work because of your brother's illness. We thought being closer to your brother would be a good situation for you. Be that as it may, it didn't work out, and we were able to put you back in the position you left here as a Journeyman pressman."

"I appreciate you bringing me back Mr. Crawford, however, how dare you send me into that kind of situation!" I then turned to Mike and said, "You know Mike, I've been through enough already, would anyone mind if I just returned to work on my regular shift and put this behind us?"

Mr. Crawford then said, "Agreed, welcome back home, and good luck."

When I left that room, I felt like my days were numbered. It was a very uncomfortable feeling, and it definitely wasn't the same kind of job it used to be with Mr. Plangere running the place. I kept my mind open, hopefully for a better offer some day, but for now, I had my family, I had my position back, a new home, and I'm safe.

The next year, I decided to concentrate on my kids even more, making sure they were growing up in the right direction. Darcy was doing great, working for a place called Tropical Fish Hobbyist (TFH). It was a small family publishing company that concentrated on selling pet books, packaged dog bones, and animal toys. Our son Michael, was in honor classes looking to attend college in the future. Unfortunately though, things weren't going as well at school with Marissa. She was just finishing up third grade and struggling with her hearing impairment. It seemed to be getting worse.

At the end of the school year, we had our annual appointment to see Dr. Sandy, Marissa's audiologist. After a thorough examination, it was determined, Marissa's hearing was deteriorating, and even more concerning was her speech had declined as well.

The test results indicated a moderate to extreme loss in both ears. Doctor Sandy showed us the reading from her hearing test. Her decibel levels were way out of the normal range and were showing about a seventy percent loss. She told us we really needed to pay close attention, these results indicate there is an extreme possibility she could go completely deaf in the future.

Her advice and plan was to have Marissa undergo aggressive speech therapy sessions, up to three times a week, and continue with sign language. Dr. Sandy also wanted Darcy and I to learn sign language too. She thought it would be beneficial for all of us to be on the same page as the loss progressed. I then asked, "Dr. Sandy, are you certain she could go completely deaf?"

"I cannot. Her impairment could stay the same or it could get worse, it's all according to her growth factor."

We took her advice and brought Marissa to therapy three times a week. Darcy and I became even more pro active because of her disability. We decided to go to a few Board of Education meetings at her school to see what assistance they could offer her. After hearing our case they suggested some changes be made to Marissa's IEP, (Individual Education Program).

A couple of months later we went to visit her teachers to see how she was progressing in the classroom. We met after school and the teachers explained to us that Marissa was having difficulties keeping up with the class. We asked why? Their reason was because of her hearing impairment. We explained to them she has an IEP that allows her extra time on her tests and preferred seating in the classroom. We asked the teachers if they were aware of her IEP. They said they were, but didn't know exactly all the content that was placed into it.

We were very upset to say the least. It seemed no teacher was experienced enough to know how to implement what was needed for Marissa to succeed. The only thing on the schools agenda was to document a program to cover the school's need to fulfill a law for a disabled student. This way, they wouldn't be liable if Marissa didn't learn in a mainstreamed school environment.

The administration assured us this program (IEP) would be the best thing for Marissa, and they would do everything they could do to assist her to be successful. We agreed, however, the program that they were trying to implement was not benefitting our daughter.

The next day we had a meeting with faculty and administration to go over what we were displeased with and how we wanted to proceed. They were very positive with us and immediately made adjustments to Marissa's IEP.

We came up with a plan to have monthly meetings on a continual basis to see how Marissa was performing in class. While preferential seating was in place, it was not totally effective for the classroom. Teachers walked around while talking and if Marissa was seated in the front of the class and a student was speaking in the back, she would not be able to hear them.

Dr. Sandy, Marissa's audiologist then came up with the idea of using a Phonic Ear System. The Phonic Ear System is where the teacher wears a microphone and Marissa wears a receiver so she can hear what the teacher is saying. With all these suggestions, we felt confident where Marissa was going to school because it seemed everyone now was really trying to assist our daughter's needs.

School finished on a good note that year and the summer was finally here.

Now it was AAU basketball season, and Riss was really excited. She started to excel in her playing abilities. We were noticing her dribbling and passing skills were getting more fluent. Her shooting technique was improving, and her hand, eye coordination skills were really developing.

I decided to advance her to competitive play and contacted a twelve year old AAU girls team called the

Howell Rebels. They were a well known team in the area that had been established for years.

I met with the coach and explained to him about Marissa's hearing impairment and he was willing to give her a try out. He said to me, at ten years old, if she could dribble and pass, I'll be happy to take her, disability or not. I told the coach, I think you'll be satisfied with her abilities.

He immediately handed her a ball and said, "Marissa, you see that that team of five players over there?"

"Yes Coach."

"You'll be playing with them and playing against that team of five on the other side." After about five minutes of play the coach then calls me over and asks, "Is she really deaf?"

Laughing, I said, "Yes, almost seventy percent."

"How is it that while dribbling the ball, she's able to turn away from people behind her and avoid having the ball stolen?"

I told him what was told to me by her audiologist. "When people have a disability with one of their senses like their eyes, ears, or even smell, the others senses kick in dramatically. What's happening is, when she feels the vibration on the floor getting stronger and closer as they approach, she has this uncanny ability to quickly sidestep away from them and they can't steal the ball from her."

He then stopped practice and instructs Marissa to go play with the first team, the one she was playing against.

When practice was over, he counted Marissa's stats. She had ten baskets, five assists and no turnovers. He then came over to me and Darcy and said, "Do me a favor guys, do not allow her to stop playing basketball, as long as she continues to play above her level, you never know where this sport is going to take her. In the meantime, I will take her and she will be starting every game for me."

That summer, Marissa was playing point guard on the Howell Lady Rebels and was averaging about twelve points a game. The summer basketball circuit was a complete success in both basketball and playing with her disability.

With summer ending, it was time for both of our children to reach new goals for the upcoming year. For our daughter, she was entering fourth grade with her new IEP, and the new performance guidelines and standards that were set into place. She received her new Phonic Ear system, courtesy of the Neptune Board of Education, which would be a device that would be a key component for her success in the main streamed environment of Woodrow Wilson school. The implementation of the Phonic Ear system made us feel confident that the school was dedicated to her achieving her academic goals. We were pleased knowing the school administration made the changes we were looking for.

As for our son Michael, he was entering his Senior year in Neptune High School as an Honor Student and a member of the Varsity Bowling team. The projections for him finding a great university for a science degree was very favorable.

At this time, Darcy was working at a new job with autistic children at the Monmouth County Learning Center for Autism, and yours truly was still working at the Asbury Park Press. Life was good, until...

Chapter XIII
Nine Eleven

What was going to happen in the coming week, no one on the face of the earth could ever be prepared for. I remember it vividly.

It was a sunny Tuesday morning when we all woke up, and the usual routines by everyone were being done. You know, showers, breakfast, and drop the kids off to school. On that day, Darcy and I were both off from work. For me, it was my usual day off, however not for Darcy. The day before, she had a miserable time at work because one of the autistic students she cared for bit her on the arm while she was teaching. It caused a break in the skin of her arm, so after receiving a tetanus shot she decided to take the next day off.

After dropping the kids off at school, we went to our usual breakfast dining spot, Carmella's Nineteenth Hole luncheonette. It was a small town breakfast joint across the street from a golf course, so the name of the luncheonette made sense. Plus it had a really good breakfast menu.

We walked in, said hi to Carmella the owner, and sat down to have breakfast at around eight thirty in the morning. It was a packed restaurant as always, and everyone was enjoying their meal, watching the television above the coffee counter.

The date was September eleventh, two thousand one, the time was eight forty-five a.m. That was the last time I looked at the clock before the first plane hit the first tower.

As my eyes were glued to the television, my thoughts immediately were like everyone else's, and then I realized we were only forty-five minutes away from the towers. I looked at Darcy and said, you know we had dinner at Windows of the World on the one hundred seventh floor of that tower last year, do you believe this!

Darcy then stares at me like fear struck her immediately! Trembling, she said, "My brother had an appointment in one of the towers today, but I don't know which one or what time!"

With a worried voice, I asked, "What's he doing there?"

With her mind racing, and her voice shaking she replied, "He sells suits to all of the executives in the towers. He gets commissions from the sales."

"Oh my God, get on the phone and call him right now!"

If we all remember, on that day, no one was getting through on any phone lines. We immediately left the diner and drove to a place called scenic point in Atlantic Highlands, New Jersey.

Scenic Point was a popular spot to go at night to make out with your date, but more so, we were thinking it was the highest peak in New Jersey and the closest view of Manhattan. We wanted to see how serious it was.

While driving there, Darcy was trying to contact her brother. It took us about thirty minutes to get to Scenic Point. As I was driving, we were listening to the radio reports.

All of a sudden, the radio announcer reported a second plane hit! We were terrified, in confusion of what was happening and not knowing what to do. The idea we had at the time, was to get to the highest point so that maybe we could get phone service, but when we arrived at the top of Scenic Point, nothing could prepare us with what we saw.

Fire and smoke was billowing over all of Manhattan. Our thought was, the entire lower island of

Manhattan could be destroyed! We couldn't believe what was happening. And still no contact with her brother.

Then Darcy said, "This is more than two planes hitting a building, I think we're getting attacked! We need to get the kids out of school!"

We then got back into the car, and hurried to the schools where our kids were. On our way, we were listening to the radio and we heard the reports that another plane crashed into the Pentagon.

Then the President came on the radio and said we were under a terrorist attack. I couldn't drive fast enough to get our kids. Darcy couldn't speed dial quick enough to get a hold of her brother. We were both thinking the worst for him because we didn't know if he was in the towers or not. We now hear on the news, the first tower went down, and still no contact with her brother.

Things were getting out of hand, now panic was all over the place, people driving frantically on the roads understandably so, no one knew what was happening. I wanted to just make sure to keep my focus on the road so I didn't get into an accident.

Finally, we arrive at Woodrow Wilson school, along with everyone else. All the parents were going in one by one frantically grabbing their kids. I get to Riss quickly and say come on, we have to pick up Michael now! Luckily, he was two minutes away and right down the road.

Darcy gets in touch with Michael on the phone and he meets us in front of the high school. I then race home, drop the kids off and tell Darcy I'm going to the Fire Department and see what their rescue plans are, or if there's anything I could do in New York City.

I arrive at the Fire Department, thinking maybe I can get on a team bus with everyone, police, fireman, and community volunteers. That would be a quick chance to get to her brother, but no such luck. New York City was temporarily shut down by Mayor Gulliani.

Our Police Chief said no one was being allowed into the city unless authorized. I then talked to the Fire Chief at the time, my friend, Bob Temple, who happened to be one of my referees in the recreation basketball league.

I told him about Darcy's brother Brett. He told me, there's no way we're getting into the city unless the Chief gives us specific orders to go. For now, I would tell Darcy to keep trying by phone, or if you know someone in the city maybe they can find out how to search for him.

I thanked Bob, told him I was heading home, and asked him to call me if he had any updated information. He wished me well and said, "Good luck with finding your brother-in-law."

When I got home, Darcy told me another plane went down in Pennsylvania.

As soon as she says that, the phone rings and it's her brother's wife Gladys, who she contacted by phone earlier. Gladys told us, Brett was on his way to the towers but got sidetracked in traffic. Presently he was walking on the Manhattan bridge with millions of others trying to get home. We were all so relieved.

As we were watching the events unfold on television, we were thinking about the lives lost, and all the families that were impacted, not knowing about their loved ones whereabouts, the condition they were in, or even if their lives perished. These events made us think about how much all of our lives were going to change forever.

We will never forget. We will never forget the first responders, the policeman, the fireman, the courageous people who put their lives before themselves to save someone else's life. May God bless all of them and may God bless all who survived and their families, as we continue to pray for them and for peace. Something this world most desperately needs RIGHT NOW. Amen.

After that horrific day, life moved on. You find a way to muddle through it by supporting each other, keeping your faith in God and hope life continues on in a more positive direction.

As for myself, I was a big New York Yankee fan, so at least there was a relief of some sadness for a few weeks until they lost the seventh game of the World Series.

As the months passed by, it was a time for healing for all of us, and for our nation. The holidays were approaching, so there was a bittersweet happiness, a change of mood that was going around for a bit. It was a time not to forget, but also a time to be grateful that your family survived the attacks knowing how others weren't as fortunate.

During those months, I was also getting updates and calls from my sister-in-law in Florida about my brother's failing health. The Hodgkin's disease was taking over my brother's body just like it took over my mom's. I knew he didn't have much time left, but I was hoping he would make the holidays, which he ended up doing, but I knew it wouldn't be much longer for him.

Sure enough, the following November I get a phone call from his wife Carol, telling me, "Tony I have bad news, I think your brother is nearing the end of his life, you better get down here right now."

That Monday, I go to my shift foreman, Al, and explain to him that I got a call last night and my brother has taken a turn for the worst, he doesn't have much time to live. Al says, "Tony, you do what you have to do, I can't guarantee what's going to happen here with your job, but you have to understand my position."

"I know Al, if it was Mr. Plangere's place, you wouldn't have even said that to me."

Al replied with sadness, "I know, I'm sorry."

At that moment, I knew it was time to get out my job. Over twenty years of a job I loved doing, it was turning my stomach now, and life, as I knew it was too short to be unhappy. My thinking was after all this is over and my brother is laid to rest, it was time to move on.

I started thinking about all the family members Darcy and I have lost, from grandparents, sisters and our moms. I started thinking about how Darcy survived breast cancer, and the intense chemotherapy and surgeries she went through to survive. There was sadness in our hearts and no matter how many times we tried to find reasons to stay in our 'ole hometown, the pain of such loses took its toll, and it was time for a fresh start.

Until we could get serious about that decision, I had to leave one more time for Tampa to be with my brother.

That day while on the plane, my first thoughts were remembering all the people from nine eleven, sitting in a plane like I am right now. I started to cry over the pain for them, and for my brother. It was an awfully sad time in my life. I started thinking about my wife, Darcy and how every day she gets up in the morning and puts her prosthesis on without ever complaining. I began to think about my mom who died the same way my brother is dying right now. I thought about my daughter who is deaf, and what life holds for her. I thought about all of our friends we had from our high school years, my bowling life, my job, our community which we loved so much. I thought about our church and Father Gerard, and how God has always been there for us, even through all our trials and tribulations, including testing our faith. But the pain in my heart was also telling me it was time to move, to a new place, a new life.

Then my plane touched down, I got my luggage and all those thoughts were put aside. It was time to focus on my brother's last days.

I arrived at his house that day and what I had seen, I had seen too many times before. Cancer has no mercy, it destroys every living part of your body in the area it decides to attack. And then it attacks the rest of the body, showing its dominant human destruction. In my brother's case, like my mother, it started in the lungs. Surely, both being heavy smokers contributed to the progress of this disease, and that's all it takes.

Memories came back to me when I was young, waking up in a small house with nine people in it, smelling the cigarette smoke everywhere. (I failed to mention whenever my brother was given money by my parents to start a new life for himself and his family, he would lose a job, a house, a bet and smoke even more cigarettes. My brother's house would be foreclosed on for no payments, but he always found a way to put a cigarette into his mouth).

I remember every time he moved out, he would buy a home and lose it again by gambling his life away and smoking cigarettes. Each time he came home, I was moved out of my bedroom. Every time this would happen, I would end up sleeping in the dining room which was right in the back of that smoke filled kitchen. Yes, getting up in the morning was like getting up to a cigarette smoking factory and I was right in the middle of it.

Everyone smoked from my dad, mom, sister-in-law, to my brother, and they all smoked those God awful Pall Mall, Marlboro filter less cigarettes. Even the Lucky Strikes with no filter in them too. I couldn't wait to get up, get ready, and go to school after that.

Yes, cigarette smoking did play a huge role in my families health and death. I guess I should of been prepared with all of them getting cancer at a young age and dying. But really, who could ever be prepared? We all have our terrible habits, some worse than others. One thing for sure though, when it's your time, it's your time. Which leads me to my brother's final moments of life.

When I arrived at his small mobile home, I saw the pain on his face. He was rolled up in a fetal position on the couch, complaining of pain in his lungs. He wasn't able to grasp air quickly enough. He was experiencing death just as my mother had experienced it. Slow agonizing breaths, minute after minute, every hour on the hour.

A man who once weighed one hundred fifty pounds down to a mere eighty. I settled in that night, knowing the outcome, and I tried to make him as comfortable as possible. Moving his body side to side on the couch relieving his pain in certain areas so he could try and sleep. I finally was able to get him somewhat comfortable and then I went to bed that night saying my prayers as usual, not knowing what the next day will bring.

Then out of nowhere that night, at four a.m. in the morning, I couldn't believe what I was seeing. My brother was standing over me on the couch, shaking my shoulder to get up. Shocked by this, I asked him, "Tom, what are you doing up?"

"Tony, my body has given me the strength one more time to have my last talk with you, I have been praying for this moment and my prayers were answered."

"Alright Tom, what do you want, you want to go somewhere? Can you walk?"

"I want to go to Wendy's and have breakfast."

I was in utter amazement! "You're hungry? You haven't eaten in days!"

"Yes I'm hungry!"

Happily, I said, "Let's go brother!"

As we were driving in the car, I asked him, "When did you get all this energy?"

Tom then said, "After I said a prayer."

132

I then said, "Funny thing brother, I've been praying since I left New Jersey hoping God would give us some time together, I guess our prayers were answered bro!"

Finally, we get to Wendy's. We got seated in a booth near the window, and he could hardly walk. Turns out he wasn't hungry, he just wanted to talk. Then he says to me, "I don't know how much more time I have left Tony, but I wanted to make sure you knew what was important to me and how I wanted my last days of life handled, and what I needed from you after that."

Hearing this filled me with sadness, but I wouldn't let him see that. "Anything Tom, spill it out, let's get to it."

First, he tells me, "I want a double plot for my wife and myself, and a military ceremony when I die."

"Okay, done."

"Then, I want you to keep an eye on my kids, don't give them any money, just listen to them, when they call you for advice, if you have the answers to their questions, I trust your judgment, let them know what you think."

"Okay, done. Anything else?"

"Yes, I want to talk to dad. We haven't been getting along for twenty-five years and I want to talk to him."

"Okay brother, that's it?"

He then said, "You were always a good brother Tony, no matter what arguments we had, I always knew I could count on you, I'm going to miss you."

Trying to hold back my tears, I said, "Look Tom, you're not dead yet. Let's go home, get some rest, and we'll handle everything."

That talk was on a Tuesday morning and lasted until eight a.m. We didn't make it home from Wendy's that day.

After leaving Wendy's, I put him into the car and he collapsed in the passenger seat. I rushed him to the hospital where he was placed in ICU. He didn't wake up again.

My brother died on Thursday, November sixteenth, two thousand two. He was fifty-six years old, two years older than our mom was when she died.

The next day, Tampa Bay Downs horse racetrack had a memorial race for him. A check for four thousand dollars was presented to his family for his military funeral, and it paid for his double plot site, as he wished.

I have kept my promise to him to this day, to be there for his kids, to listen to them and guide them in any way that I can.

By the time I was forty years old, another one of our family members gone to cancer. That made two sister-in-laws, a brother, two moms and a wife who almost lost her life to that disease. When the day was done, I called Darcy and our sentiments were the same, it was time to move on from our beloved home in New Jersey.

My mom and dad on my brother's wedding day, 1967.

My mom, grand-mom, and me, 1967.

My brother Tom on my wedding day, 1980.

The Casper family, 1972.

Darcy and my wedding
day, 1980

Bowling as a senior in high
school, 1977

My mom and I on my wedding day, 1980.

Darcy and I, 1980.

My mother-in-law, with Kathy and Michele, 1977.

Michael, Grand-
Pop and I 1987.

Marissa, in the garage dribbling, 1997.

Mr. Plangere, Owner Asbury Park Press

Disney World,
after cancer,
1997.

Family's cancer legacy moves teen to ponder genetic testing

By ANNE GEGGIS
STAFF WRITER

DELTONA — The hair, the clothes, the makeup: Darcy Cimino looks at her daughter and sees her older sister, Kathryn, all over again.

But there's one way that she's hoping Marissa doesn't resemble Kathryn, or her eldest sister, Michele, or her, for that matter.

All three women, two of them dead before age 40, were born with a gene mutation that makes it almost

DARCY CIMINO   MARISSA CIMINO

inevitable — up to an 85 percent chance — that a particularly aggressive form of breast cancer will develop over a lifetime.

"Now that she's older, I think about it a lot," said Cimino, 49. Marissa, who turned 17 this

For those with a pronounced family history like Marissa's, the testing — which uses less than 2 teaspoonfuls of blood to peer at the raw materials of who we are — has come out of scientists' labs to become the stuff of television commercials. For the first time since 2005, when hereditary cancer testing became available in this area, a direct-to-patient ad campaign has hit the airwaves.

More insurance companies are covering the $3,900 test that's an outgrowth of the Human Genome Project, which completed in 2003, identified about 25,000 to 40,000 genes in our body.

Through the manufacture of proteins for the cell, these genes govern how each cell among trillions of cells in our body behaves

Marissa's 1st Holy Communion with Father Gerard, 1999.

Marissa with Vivian Stringer, North Carolina, 2006.

Sophomore Year, 2007

Daytona Beach News Journal, 2007.

Michael's graduation from the University of Delaware, 2006.

Marissa, Hollins University, 2010.

Marissa, Carnival Cruise Lines, Alaskan Cruise, 2013.

Chapter XIV
The New Move

We were concentrating on Florida as the new place to live and from all the pain we endured from cancer, twelve hundred miles away seemed far enough.

After my brother's death, the first thing on the list when I got home was to find a newspaper job in Florida. The Orlando Sentinel looked like a good choice. It was an established company with no union disputes.

A week after I sent my resume and application to the Orlando Sentinel, I received a call back from their Human Resources Department and they wanted to meet me.

Over the next few months I made a couple of visits back and forth, met with personnel and the staff and decided to take the job. They offered me a position to work on this new high tech printing press machine. It was a new press they wanted to run because demand was high on advertisement revenue and this two million dollar machine would be the answer to their problems.

The only problem I had was the position only paid half the salary I was making in New Jersey, welcome to Florida. My thoughts were, with the sale of the house and my 401k package I might be able to afford this move. We were all very excited about it. I even let my brother's kids know we would be a little closer to them and they were ecstatic. It seemed like a great move.

The next thing on the list was to inform my hometown community of our decision to relocate. I informed the Board of Education, Board of Recreation, and town council of our intentions, this way they would have ample time to find a replacement for all the volunteer positions I soaked up into my life.

We also let Marissa's school know because we needed all her IEP information for her new school in Florida. As for my son, he was accepted into the University of Delaware and was into his sophomore year of college completing his education endeavors.

As far as my job at the Asbury Park Press, well, I wasn't going to tell them anything until I was ready.

We knew we were moving, however, we didn't want to disrupt any normal activities in Marissa's life, especially basketball, since it was very important to her. She was currently playing AAU basketball for the Colts Neck Cloverleaf's, a twelve year old team that would play higher level competitive teams because the players all had goals to play in high school. This team was perfect for Marissa.

I immediately made the coach aware of her impairment. Right away, he wanted to check her skills out, from dribbling, to passing, and shooting abilities. He then ran her through some more technical drills and decided to put her on the bench.

For about five minutes, the first team and second team were out there playing. He decides to stop practice and moves Marissa onto the first team to play a full game with them. My thinking was, he probably wanted to give her a glimpse of what was out there and what she had to contend with. It didn't take the coach very long to be impressed. When the game was over, she scored twenty-one points and had about eleven assists. The players were stunned that she couldn't hear, and they couldn't figure out how she was not getting the ball stolen.

The coach called the team over after the game and said to the girls, "If she can play like this being deaf, then there's no reason not to expect more off yourselves!"

Then a player asked, "Marissa, how do you know where everyone is on the court behind you?"

After reading her lips, Marissa said, "I can feel all of you from the vibrations on the floor. As you get closer, the vibration gets stronger, so I just move to the side quickly to see where you're at!"

Then the same player asked, "How did you know what I just asked you?"

"Riss," as I call her, then told them all, "I can hear, but I can also read lips, the only problem I really have is like the one I have in the classroom at school. When two people talk at the same time, it's almost impossible for me to know what you guys are talking about."

Another player then asked, "How do you talk so well?"

"When I was three years old, my mom and dad threw me into speech therapy. They doubled the amount of sessions and gave me more time to spend with the therapist. At that time I was only about forty percent deaf and I was able to get more help with my speaking. The more time I put in, the better my speech got." She went on to say, "Being eleven years old, I'm about seventy percent deaf now, but because I was as able to hear then, it made it easier for me now. Another problem that I have is, when my hair is down, people don't even realize I'm deaf, they can't see my hearing aids, but it's okay, I feel like one of you guys."

After she spoke to them, the team, coaches, parents and players were completely in awe of her. They came up to Darcy and I and wanted to know how this happened, and what we did to get her where she was at today. That was the first time ever that players and coaches asked *her* questions about her impairment.

Then, something amazing happened for the first time ever, and it set a precedence for years to come for the rest of her basketball career.

The coach assembles the team in a circle and says, "Guess what? We have a new secret weapon guys." Everyone looked around at each other and were trying to figure out what he was thinking. Then the coach said, "Our secret weapon is Marissa. Not only for her ability to play basketball, but her ability to play being hearing impaired."

The team looked at each other thinking, this coach is crazy! He went on to say to them, "From now on girls, when we run the plays, we choose what play we run by our face."

He turned to one of his players, Lindsay and asked her, "What's the color of your lips?"

Lindsay replied, "Red Coach."

"Okay, the play for Alabama is now Red, as in the color of your lips, so when you run that play, point to your lips and everyone will know it's Alabama. Silence is deadly."

He calls to another player and yells, "Kelly! What color are your eyes?"

Kelly yells back, "Blue Coach."

"The play Tennessee is now Blue, just point to your eyes."

Then he asked, "Team, what color is your face."

They all looked at each other and yelled out, "Brown. Tan. Yellow. White." Everyone started to laugh.

As for Darcy and I, we were overwhelmed with emotion seeing that everyone was responding in a positive way to her handicap.

Then the coach tells the team, "All the colors you yelled out for your face, those will be our defensive plays! No team we play against will be able to figure out what play we're running! Now let's get to work."

I went over to the coach, called him a genius, and hugged him. I couldn't thank him enough for such a brilliant idea. That year, the Colts Neck Cloverleaf's went

13-1, their best record ever. Marissa's play at point guard was so impressive, high school coaches were coming up to us and asking where she will be attending high school.

On the hometown community front, in March of two thousand three, recreation basketball season was just finishing up. After the season is over, we have are annual Awards Night for the kids, parents and volunteers who helped run the league. Normally hundreds of people would show up in the gym for the festivities, but this year it looked like a thousand people showed up.

Players, parents, coaches, referees, you name it, they were there. I guess when word got out we were moving, they were expecting a big crowd in the gym that night to show their support for our family.

The day before the Awards Night, Bill Folk, the school administrator for Woodrow Wilson elementary school called me in to his office and said, "Tony, I think it would be a good idea to have a great closing speech ready for tomorrow night."

"Come on Bill."

"No, I'm not kidding, they're expecting a capacity crowd in the gym of over a thousand people, and the gym only holds about twelve hundred."

I couldn't believe what I was hearing. Then he said, "Because you mean so much to this community, we are going to lift the fire code to allow everyone to attend, so have your speech ready!"

I immediately went home and told Darcy about the news and she was filled with emotion, as we all were. My daughter Marissa said jokingly, "Dad you better have a good speech ready!"

On that cold Tuesday night in March, Bill Folk turned out to be right. I couldn't even find a parking place. The event was to start at seven p.m. and I think the entire town got there at six! There were well over a thousand people in that gym that night.

Darcy went into the double doors first with Marissa. As they walked in, they started clapping for them, then as I approached it only got louder, then they started to chant, Tone-Simone! Tone-Simone, over and over again.

I was overwhelmed by the sincere appreciation and love in that building. I mean, other than the day I got married, my kids being born, and the Ernest W. Lass Award, it was probably the most exciting thing that ever happened to me.

The Mayor at the time was Thomas Arnone. Mr. Arnone, council members from town, the police, fireman, EMT'S and the Public Works department were all there to show their support for me and my family. After a few minutes when the standing room only audience calmed down, the council members presented me with a plaque for all the outstanding volunteer work I did for the community of Neptune City. It was an amazing night!

When I finished my speech, and the night was over, not a single person left the building until they shook my hand, gave me a hug or just wished me well on our new endeavor. I made sure I told everyone there that night, I will never ever forget the people, the school, the community, administration, police and fireman of Neptune City, New Jersey.

Finally, our house sold and it was now time to tell the Asbury Park Press newspaper I was leaving after twenty-one years of service.

I approached my foreman, Al Truax to speak with him about how difficult the last few years have been. I explained to him how the last transfer down to Ft. Myers was so stressful on my family it deterred our plans, I guess it just wasn't time to move yet. I also explained how blessed and fortunate I was for my job here, the people in my life, and how difficult it was to make this decision.

I told him, "I have decided to resign my position and hand in my two week notice."

Al then said, "Tony, I knew your resignation was coming soon. It has been a pleasure to be your boss and your friend. I enjoyed all those years playing tennis with you after work. I enjoyed all those company picnics and softball games you put together for us, but most of all, I can't thank you enough for showing your humility and professionalism in the worst of times in life. I have total respect for you and your family's decision. But, if you don't mind, I want you to wait to tell the guys in the pressroom about your leaving. It's seven thirty a.m., can we wait until ten when its coffee break? I want to get the guys together in the coffee room and have you tell them yourself. They would want to hear this directly from you. So go back to work, I'll see you in the coffee room later."

"No problem, thank you Al."

My best friends, Tom Casper, Gene Lewis and Sam D'Agostino already knew about what was going on and they wanted to meet in the locker room after my meeting with Al. When my meeting was finished, we all met and I told them Al wanted me to break the news to everyone at ten o'clock in the break room. Their response was, is there going to be donuts in there! That response was typical of any pressman.

At ten o'clock, about fifty pressman, plate room people, machinists and paper handlers gathered in the coffee room. When I saw Al at the door of the break room, I turned to him and said jokingly, "What did you do, tell everybody in the building?"

He smirked and said, "Come on man, this is the newspaper, the gossip in here is worst than outside on the streets!"

We both went into the coffee room and it was kind of like a usual meeting, only thing was people were looking at me wondering why I came in with Al. Al then said, "Tony has something he would like to talk to you all about."

I told the guys it was a pleasure working here over twenty years with all of you, but I just gave my two week notice. My family and I are relocating to Florida and I will be working with a different company.

When the meeting was finished, every single person in that room wished me the best for my life. It was a special moment, very quiet and solemn.

Some of the guys after the meeting came up to me and said, "We had a feeling you were going to leave, we said of all people, you would be the first not to put up with all that corporate bull crap. That stuff is going to be around here for a long, long time. I'm sure Mr. Plangere would be very proud of your decision. We all know you did this because of him not being here Tony."

That moment made me feel like it was the right decision.

On my last day of work at the Asbury Park Press, Al brought me down to the Personnel/Human Resources Department for my exit interview. I found out why the new company called it an exit interview. It's because Gannett wanted to hear any dirt you had to offer so they could use it towards that employee later on.

The first question Human Resources asked me was, "Do you have any complaints working for Gannett Corporation?"

I sarcastically said, "Do you want to go over the transfer where you guys sent me down to a union dispute, or do you want to talk about the twenty years of my relationship with Mr. Plangere?"

At that moment, they shut the questioning down and said, "Well, as long as you're on the Mr. Plangere train, I guess we should give you this."

"What's that?" I asked, as they handed me an envelope.

"Mr. Plangere and the Asbury Park Press left this envelope aside for you and we were told to give it to you on the day of your resignation."

I shook their hand in disgust and left, wondering what was in the envelope.

I then went back upstairs to the pressroom and said my final goodbyes and wished everyone well.

When I got outside to my car I couldn't wait to open up the envelope to see what Mr. Plangere left for me. Inside, there was a letter expressing his gratitude for my years of service, and that I would receive a check from his grandfathered account in the amount of thirty-five thousand dollars!

I can't explain how I felt. It was euphoria, gratefulness and humility at the same time. I couldn't believe it, but then knowing Mr. Plangere, it was believable, he was one of the most generous, thoughtful, giving, compassionate men I ever met in my life.

Another moment of knowing I made the right decision, or, at least I thought at the time.

Thank you Mr. P.

Chapter XV
Know Your Strengths

When I got home that day, I couldn't wait to tell Darcy the story about the coffee room and exit interview. I then showed her the letter I received from Mr. Plangere. She broke down in tears. She couldn't believe Mr. P who used to call her up on Sunday mornings to see how she was feeling after her chemo treatments would do this. She said, "When we get to Florida, we're going to have to look him up for a visit."

"How?" I asked.

"I did some research, turns out, he has a place down in south Florida."

I laughed and said, "You are a smart wife, aren't you."

"Hey, you married me, does that make you smarter?"

"Um no." I said laughing and gave her a big hug.

We were very busy packing up our home, so after a very toned down Christmas, we were now preparing ourselves to leave. Everything was going according to schedule.

It was a cold, snowy day out, and like every morning, we do the same ritual, get the coffee ready, make some breakfast, let our dog out.

We had a beautiful pure bread ten year old "Lassie" collie. Her name was Daisy. We would usually let her out the back door onto the deck I built. Our Daisy, like most dogs, especially collies, when they get old, their back legs and hips get weak and arthritis sets in, so it's very difficult for them to get up and down the stairs.

That day, it was cold outside with about eight inches of snow on the deck, and she couldn't make it down the stairs. She kept standing at the patio door to come in and wouldn't go down. I told the kids to let her in, and we would put her out through the front door today. Daisy was a very smart dog, and if we had to put her out through the front door, she never went near the street.

My son, Michael was on winter recess from Delaware at the time, and all of a sudden, out of nowhere, I hear him yell Daisy! I then heard a loud screech!

I run from the patio to the front door, and I see a large truck pulled over to the side of the road and I see our collie, our Daisy, laying still in the middle of the road.

I immediately ran to her side and noticed her eyes were still open, but a trickle of blood coming out from her mouth. Just then, a car pulls up and it happens to be Caryn, Michaels girlfriend. She starts going hysterical yelling what happened? Michael goes over and consoles her, and then he gets Darcy from inside the house. She had no idea what was going on.

Darcy runs outside after hearing the news and she starts to scream at the truck driver. The truck driver didn't speak very good English, but seeing how he was getting yelled at, he decided to drive off. I then turn to Darcy and said, "Forget him! We have to get Daisy to the vet."

We wrapped her up in a blanket and we both lifted her into the back of our Jeep Grand Cherokee. We made it to the vet in about twenty minutes.

They immediately brought her in. The vet, Dr. Webber, then has me lay her on the table and she examines Daisy.

After examining her, Dr. Webber looks at me and Darcy and says, "Your dog has broken bones, fractured ribs, a punctured lung, and massive internal injuries. She is to the point where an operation would be totally unsuccessful, I'm sorry."

We both look at each other and know what's going to happen next. Darcy says to me, "When we get home, we will have a talk with the kids, there's nothing we can do for Daisy."

Dr. Webber looked at both of us and said, "I'm going to prepare what I need to do next for Daisy, are you both alright?"

I said, "Doctor, if I had a dollar for every time a doctor said that to me in my life."

Dr. Webber then said, "I'm sorry. I'll be right back."

When the needle was put into our Daisy, we both watched her eyes close slowly and as her breaths grew deeper and deeper into a sleep, all I kept thinking about was, human or animal, we all have one short life to live and how precious life is and no matter what, our breaths that we breathe, are so valuable. No dollar amount we earn can stop the inevitable when it's our time. Then our Daisy died.

While hugging our Daisy after she died, Dr. Webber was listening to stories about our life and she couldn't believe what we've been through. She wished us well, gave us a hug and said, "We'll take it from here."

When I went to pay the bill, the clerk at the counter said, "Doctor said, no charge. Good luck on your move."

We went home, hugged our kids, and said, we were lucky to have Daisy as long as we did, she was very ill the last couple years of her life. Michael then turns to me and says, "But Dad, a truck! Come on man! I hope this is not a sign of things to come!"

"Michael, I have no answers for what happened today or for anyone else who passed away in our family. All I know is, when you're on this earth and when you leave this earth, you put your life into God's hands and with the experience and faith both your mom and I have, I can tell you unequivocally without hesitation, God will be there for you, *always*! I can guarantee that."

When Christmas and winter recess was over, we drove Michael back to school in Delaware to finish his sophomore year. It was then time to get the moving truck ready and head down to Orlando, Florida.

I had made arrangements for us to stay at the Extended Stay hotel for a couple of months, giving us time to look for a new home outside the Orlando area.

While I was starting my first day of work at the Orlando Sentinel, Darcy was trying to find a school and an area to live.

It was the usual first day, I met with personnel, went to orientation, signed all the necessary documents, insurance, tax papers, and so on. Then I was escorted to the Small Press Advertisement Department. There is where I met my supervisor, Wendy and her assistant Mike. The Small Press Advertisement Department was in charge of all minor advertising printing, such as: coupon books, TV guides, business flyers, and small circulars that went into the Sunday newspaper.

While I was printing the coupon books and TV guides on the small printing press, Mike was working on the new high tech two million dollar printing press. This high tech press was the printing machine the personnel department mentioned to me during my phone interview and was the reason why they hired me in the first place. I was told their agenda was to immediately get me trained on this high tech press for the up and coming advertising jobs. From my experience and knowledge with printing machines, it seemed like a quality piece of equipment that could do magnificent color work for large commercial jobs. Only problem was, I never got to work on it.

In the meantime, I was asked to work on the small press unit they had in the shop. Starting the press up, I noticed the rubber roller ink train that supports ink to the paper for proper printing purposes was oscillating back and forth in an irregular way. The printing was very muddy on the paper, sort of like double vision to the reader.

Several times during the day, I advised Mike, Wendy's assistant, about the problem I was having with the rollers. At first, he looked like he could care less. I continued to explain to Mike, the ink roller train on the machine is operating irregularly, and I asked him, "Do you have a maintenance man that comes out to recalibrate these rollers any time soon?"

His reply to me was, "Tony, how long have you been working on presses?"

"Over twenty-two years."

He then said to me coyly, "Well if you have that much experience, I think you should have the knowledge and experience to fix it yourself, right?"

"I guess you guys do things differently here. Back home we had machinists that would come in when called upon and they would replace, recalibrate and repair the settings on those rollers automatically for us."

"Welcome to Florida." he replied sarcastically, then turned and walked away.

Then my boss Wendy comes over to get the job I was working on. When she grabs the pile of proofs, she looks at me and said angrily, "These aren't any good! The ink and setting on them are muddy!"

"Wendy, I'm going to tell you the same thing I told Mike."

When I told her the same story, she said, "Maybe you're not the guy we're looking for."

In disbelief, I then turned and walked away from her.

When the day was over, I went home thinking, what am I supposed to do with this job if things don't work out?

During dinner, I explained the entire story to Darcy and Marissa. When I was done, Darcy said, "There are two things I'm wondering about here, first how long has Mike been in that department, and secondly, what if you called

160

back home to see if you could get your job back in New Jersey? I can't believe that happened to you on your first day! What kind of welcoming is that for a new employee?"

"Hopefully things get better hun, how did your day go?"

"Well mine went a little better than yours. I found a place to live and a middle school for Marissa, the only problem is, there's not a lot of support down here for her disability. Everywhere I went the schools are in desperate need for grants, and federal funding dollars. But I do like a particular school."

After my experience with my first day of work, hearing what Darcy was saying about the Florida schools, it didn't surprise me. "I guess we'll just have to advocate a little more for her needs, you know the old saying, "the squeaky wheel is the one that gets the oil."

Then Darcy said, "As for your day, keep your eye on that guy Mike. It sounds like he's threatened by your knowledge, position and experience, and may be feeling his job might be in jeopardy. Don't expect any help from him."

By the second day, third day, and fourth day at work, Darcy was right, things didn't get any better with the machines, Wendy or Mike. However, I actually found a way to repair those oscillating rollers and the press started to print quality work. Even my boss Wendy came up to me and said, "Now I know why you were so highly recommended by your supervisors back in Jersey. You are a consummate professional printer."

The weeks went by and now it was May. The weather was getting hot, something we weren't accustomed to. After months of searching, Darcy called me while I was at lunch and said excitedly, "Tony, I found a new home! It's in a town called Deltona. It's a large town and they are updating the infrastructure and new home developments are being built everywhere."

161

"That's fantastic!"

Darcy continued, "I researched all the middle schools in the area and found out Deltona Middle had one of the highest ratings in the county. While on a tour at the school and talking to other parents, you'll never believe what happened! During a conversation, I met a high school basketball coach. His name is Bruce Palmer. He came up to me and said he overheard a conversation I was having about Marissa playing basketball in New Jersey. He told me he was the head coach of Pine Ridge High School girls basketball team. They are a cross-town rival of Deltona High school. He also told me that most of the middle school girls basketball players attend Deltona Middle school, but when they graduate, they have the option to choose Deltona High School or Pine Ridge High School, where he coaches. I told him our daughter has been playing since she's been five years old and that we would hopefully be talking to him soon about her career."

"Wow," I said. "God works in mysterious ways."

A few days later I called Darcy on my lunch break to see how her day was going. Darcy told me, "After I picked Riss up at school, I started to drive around to look for basketball courts in the area. I found this park that had basketball courts outside the recreation center, and it's about ten minutes from the house. While Riss was playing, this guy comes over to me, and guess what? It was the same guy, that coach, from Deltona Middle school! He told me he had been watching her play ball and the boys she was playing with were eight graders and he said she was dominating them! He was asking if we would be willing to send her to Pine Ridge High School after Deltona Middle school. Isn't that great! So I told him I would talk to you about it."

I told Darcy, "Next time you see him, give him our phone number."

"Tony, while we were talking he met Marissa and he didn't even know she was hearing impaired."

I laughed and said, "No worries, her disability never stopped her before." We were both so excited about that conversation with the coach, it seemed we made the right choice where to live.

When I finally got home that night, the first thing Darcy asked was how my day went. I told her its going better, Wendy said some nice things to me today. She then asked, "Have you started printing on that new tech machine yet?"

"Hell no! They haven't even trained me on it!"

"Wasn't that machine the reason why they hired you?"

Shaking my head, I told her, "Yes I thought so, but it sure doesn't seem that way."

"What about Mike? Is he working on it?"

"Yes, every day."

"Maybe you should have a talk with Wendy tomorrow about it. There has to be a reason why you're not being trained."

I agreed, "That's a good idea."

The following day, I arrive at work thirty minutes early. Wendy was already there, so I approached her and asked if we could have a talk. She replied, "Sure."

I told her, "I really appreciate the compliment you gave me the other day. How about giving me a chance on that tech press, that is the reason why you hired me, right?"

"Mike is the one who is supposed to train you."

"Okay, but three weeks have gone by and not once, have I touched that machine."

"Well, Mike is on vacation for the next three weeks, so it doesn't look like you're going to get to work on it anytime soon."

Thinking how ridiculous this was, I then asked, "What about all the ad jobs that are scheduled to run?"

"Tony, we back-logged them until Mike gets back."

"Isn't that kind of counterproductive?" I asked.

She then abruptly said, "Tony, this discussion is over! You have many jobs to run on the small press over the next three weeks. You would have been too busy to be trained anyway, so I think this is the best course of action to take."

Confused, I asked, "What do you mean? You have a two million dollar machine sitting there with no jobs to be printed on it?"

Again she says, "This meeting is over!"

I immediately started to think, is this guy Mike not showing me because I'm a threat to him, like Darcy said? Or are they trying to get me to quit or resign because of him? I now was suspicious of everything, and knew from that moment on something was being kept from me.

Now I started to get a little worried about my position there. I drove home that night thinking twice about talking to Darcy about it because she was so happy about the house, the school and meeting the coach, so I decided to discuss it another time.

When I got home, Darcy couldn't wait to greet me at the door with some good news. She said, "Honey I know things aren't going so well for you right now at your job but your son called today and he made the Dean's list! On top of that, I got a job! It's at a Catholic School, called All Souls and it's only fifteen minutes from our house. It's beautiful, has a wonderful church, and the job has a full benefits package."

I told her, "That's great news. I'm so happy Michael is doing well at school. And getting a job at a catholic school is what you always wanted, I'm happy for you."

Then she added, "I forgot to mention, that coach from Pine Ridge High School called up today and wanted to talk to you about Riss."

After hearing all that great news, I knew I made a good choice not to tell her about my day. After dinner, I called Coach Palmer for the first time.

He immediately started raving about Marissa's basketball abilities. It was like a college coach recruiting her. He told me, she shoots threes, passes like Larry Bird, and rebounds like Charles Oakley on the Knicks, where did you find her! I started laughing, then I said, "That's nice coach, but I have to tell you one thing that's going to make you tilt back in your chair a little."

Concerned, he said, "Oh no, you're not choosing another school are you?"

"No coach, she's hearing impaired."

He then said, "Excuse me? I didn't get that."

I repeated, "Coach, she's hearing impaired, she can't hear very well."

All of a sudden it got quiet on the phone, then I hear him asking his daughter, Paige, did you know she was deaf? "Coach?" I repeated "Coach? Are you there?"

Finally, he gets back on the phone, apologizes for his rudeness and says, "I'm blown away man! I would of never figured that out. How did she learn to play like that?"

"Like normal kids do. Practice, practice, practice."

He then tells me, "I love her, and I want her to play for me. We have an eighth grade AAU Team that will be playing down at Disney in a couple of weeks. This Saturday we're having a team practice, can she attend?"

"Absolutely."

The Friday before practice, we closed mortgage on our home and I was so relieved I made it through another work week, all the while, praying that it would get better there in the near future.

165

That Saturday morning, we dropped Marissa off at Pine Ridge High School for her first AAU practice. When we returned a few hours later, Coach Palmer approached us and said, "Your daughter was incredible. She was scoring at will, getting players involved and running the floor. Before I could even get the play out, she knew exactly what to do out there. She is going to be an incredible basketball player! And oh, by the way, we're on that color code face system, the same one her old coach figured out."

"She told you about that?"

"Yes," he said. "It was easy for the players to pick up, only difference is our plays are a little more involved and difficult, but she's a quick learner. I still can't believe she's hearing impaired."

Again, I was blown away with the positive energy and compassion they all displayed as a team. The next week at Disney the team put in a modest showing, it was expected knowing Riss was new to the offense and only two weeks in, but she impressed her team so much they couldn't wait to play together in high school. It was a great weekend of basketball.

Now, it's Monday morning, and I'm back at work, and finally, Mike, is back from vacation. Immediately, I approached him and asked, "Hey Mike, how about getting me started on that tech machine today. This way when you're out sick or on vacation we won't lose any jobs that come in."

He just looks at me and walks away. I said, "Excuse me Mike, please don't disrespect me like that and walk away, be a man and just tell me what's up."

He turns to me and said, "Look, let's get something straight New York guy."

"Correction, I'm from Jersey, so you got that one wrong already."

Arrogantly, Mike responded, "Whatever. This is my machine, that little one over there, that one is yours. If Wendy needs you on this machine, she'll let you know about it, in the meantime back off!"

"How does she plan for me to work on that press, when I'm not even trained on it?"

"I don't know, take that up with her." He then walked out of the room.

At that moment, Wendy comes into the room and I approached her quickly about this problem. She turned to me and said, "I just finished a meeting about your printing time numbers, and we noticed most of your times are not done in the specific amount of time we demand. This is causing paper waste and ink waste. I didn't want to throw this on you because I'm sure with your relocating and all, you have enough pressure on you already. In the meantime, there were a few nights I had to ask Mike to stay late and finish up some products you printed in a unprofessional manner."

Shocked, I said, "Excuse me? Why wasn't I told about this sooner? That pressure reason is no excuse not to tell me Wendy."

Wendy continued, "Everything has been documented, and right now, I don't want to discuss this situation any further because my dog is dying at home and I'm not in a good frame of mind to continue this conversation." I dismissed the conversation as she requested and didn't pursue the issue any further.

On my way home that night, I started asking myself when and how I was going to get fired from this job. I entered the house and I must have had this look of disgust on my face, because immediately Darcy asked me, "Did you get fired today?"

I said sarcastically, "How did you guess?" Then rolling my eyes, I said, "No, not yet."

I did tell Darcy about what happened, even about Wendy's dog. I felt real bad about that. She then said, "Tony it seems to me they want to get you to resign, like you're in the way of something they want to do."

"I think you might be right, but why then did they hire me in the first place? I have Wendy's phone number, I think I'm going to give her call and ask about her dog."

Darcy then said, "I wouldn't do that if I were you!"

I disagreed. "I felt bad about our conversation today, it's her dog, she said he was dying. I'm not going to ask her about anything else."

"Tony I understand how you feel, but it's your boss, the one who seems to me, never takes your side, I wouldn't."

I called her anyway.

When Wendy answered the phone, I immediately asked her how her dog was doing. The only words that came out of her mouth were, "Fine, don't call here again." She then hung up.

I thought to myself, darn, I should of listened to Darcy.

The next day at work, I get called into the Human Resources Department. Upon arriving at Human Resources, Wendy was there to greet me at the door. I asked, "What's going on?"

She replied, "We're having a meeting today."

"Is it about me and the phone call to you last night?" I asked her.

"I'm not at liberty to discuss it right now."

I said, "Fine."

As Wendy and I walked down the hall, to the meeting room, we passed a room with a bunch of people in there who looked like lawyers. The meeting room we were in was adjacent to that room.

As I walked in, Wendy left. I looked around the room and all the Human Resource managers are there and no one from my department was present. Then a security guard shows up. My thought was, they're either going to ask me to resign, or force me to quit.

As we all sit down, the first question asked was, "Tony, did you call Wendy at home last night?"

"Yes, I asked about her dog. Why, are you going to fire me for that?"

"No," they said. "We're not going to fire you."

"Then why are we having this meeting? Did I do something wrong on your two million dollar tech machine. You know, the one I never got trained on? What's this meeting all about?"

"From the first day you worked here, there has been a conflict of interest in your department. It seems Mike and you haven't been working well together, and we had concerns because you called Wendy at home last night. Plus recently, some work you printed was done incorrectly and you put your department over budget. What do you have to say about that?"

"I called Wendy about her dog out of concern and compassion, prior to that, I was asking her why I was never trained on the tech machine. She would say, she didn't want to discuss the matter, it was the same day she brought up her dog. The second matter you questioned was Mike. I never had a problem with Mike, heck, he was on vacation for three weeks so I hardly talked to the guy. When I did, he threatened me saying things like, no one from Jersey is going to touch this machine! And the third thing you asked, was about my numbers, and I can't answer that, because I was never confronted about the situation until I asked Wendy about getting trained. Prior to that I never heard a thing about it, so what exactly is going on here, an investigation into nothing?"

169

Their reply was, "Tony you weren't what we expected. We didn't think you needed training, and you have been confrontational. We think it would be a good idea if you resigned without notice."

Angrily, I said, "Excuse me? I'm not going to resign. I can't believe what I'm hearing. These accusations are lies, and I want to know who demanded this meeting!"

"Tony, we have instructions from our publisher to sever this relationship with you today. As you know, this is a right to hire, right to fire state, therefore, we don't need a reason, we thought it would be best just to have you resign."

I then said, "I have done nothing wrong but show up for work every day on time. I always presented myself in a professional manner. I was never late coming back from lunch, and I never used abusive language, like some people I know. According to myself, and Wendy at times, I was getting my work done in a timely manner, and what's irritating about this is that I'm looking at all of you people right now, and not one of you comes close to the amount of years of experience I have in the newspaper business. You, over there, it looks like you just got out of college! You, over there, have you ever printed on a printing press before? How many of you are even married longer than five years? I bet none of you. How many of you even attend church regularly?"

I was then interrupted, and one of them asked, "What is it you want from us Tony?"

"A fair deal, without prejudice, or lies. To do my job, to be trained on a machine that I was hired to print on. Just an honest day's work for an honest day's dollar. And, I'll tell you something else, there's no way I'm stepping down from this job. You're going to have to fire me to get rid of me."

Then there was a pause, and an opening for them to do what they came to do. The Human Resources Director then said, "Fine, Tony, as of today you are terminated. Hand in your badge, you are not allowed back on these premises."

"Fine." I said. "Two things before I leave."

Snidely the Human Resources Director replied, "What?"

"First, what exactly are you firing me for? I'm at least entitled to know that. And secondly, will you be able to approve my unemployment today? I'm going to have to use that for the first time in my life."

"Yes, you will get your unemployment."

"Okay, and what's the reason for termination?"

They said, "You called Wendy, your boss at home and asked her about her dog, that was harassment."

Banging my hands down on the table, I yelled, "Oh come on, give me a break! You said in the beginning of the meeting that wasn't going to be the reason."

Then the meeting was abruptly adjourned. Security escorted me down to the front desk and that was it. Funny thing, about two years later, I learned the real reason why I was terminated.

One night, while we were on our way to Orlando to watch a Magic basketball game, I wanted to drive by the Sentinel newspaper and check out where I used to work. As we approached the corner of the building, my old office looked desolate. The small printing department that I worked in was shut down, and that two million dollar tech machine in the corner, well it had cob webs over it to the point where Spiderman could probably sleep on them. So much for the newspaper business.

Chapter XVI
The Mop

    While I walked out of the Orlando Sentinel, after being terminated that day, for the first time since I was young, I was feeling an emptiness, a feeling of being a failure. That was an emotion I rarely have ever felt. I mean, I always had a job, I was responsible for lives, other than myself, to take care of and support.

    I remember while driving home, after that dreadful meeting, I began to think how it must feel for so many people who lose their job. It's devastating to your morale, heart and mind, and that can really play tricks on you. Being terminated made me question myself, I was scared, wondering if I could get another job.

    I now had an understanding how it could affect other people who had been disappointed, or failed in something that was so important to them. I thought about people who had been terminated in a way like myself, and had no answers on how or why it happened. Some people get so distraught, they even contemplate suicide. It's a shame this can really happen to any of us at some point in our lives. For some people, it could be even more devastating because there may be no one there to support them. You can feel alone, ashamed, distraught, angry, embarrassed, to the point where you start to question your own self worth.

    Then I thought about the people who feel like, oh well, in a nonchalant attitude and think, no worries for me, I'll get another job. Or the ones who think, well, I always have my unemployment check to fall back on.

    For most people though, a job is a sense of pride, self worth, importance, confidence, and responsibility. A job is about earning your own way, a self accomplishment and not having to ask anyone for anything. It's building a frame of mind to earn status in your life and feeling good about yourself for what you do and taking pride in doing it. That's what a job is all about.

As for me, the day I was fired, was humbling, an eye opener, it made me realize how lucky I was to have a job all my life. I was humbled, not angry after that meeting.

A sudden sense of actual calm, not fear, came over me. That's what God does for you if you have faith in Him. It did for me that day. Yes, it was a death of a job, but that was it, it was just a job. Now, I would be lying if I didn't say while driving home that day I wasn't nervous about talking to my wife, Darcy. But, in my mind, I had this feeling, this sense, that everything happens for a reason and not to worry. Many times I have felt this way, I have prayed and my prayers have been answered. I knew this was God's way of helping me move onto another venture in my life.

Then I said, "Wait! I just got fired!" But the anger, devastation, sorrow, instability just wasn't there. I felt God had my back and whatever was going to happen, it was going to be okay.

I then pulled up in front of our house and Darcy was waiting for me outside. She had been watering the flowers. The look must have been written all over my face. I said to her, "Did I give it away?"

"I know you like a book, you're not the kind of man to cry from personal adversity, you got fired didn't you?"

"Yup."

"All over that dog right?"

"Yup." Then we both then started to laugh.

I guess from all the years of adversity, losing close relatives to cancer, Darcy going through it herself, Marissa's hearing impairment, leaving the newspaper, going down to Ft. Myers and getting harassed, and now getting fired, you start to build a protective wall of

173

immunity around your body. This way, you're prepared when someone hurts you mentally.

Your strength of failures, become just that, more strength, and a way to cope better. The adversities you've dealt with, learned mistakes, seeing family die right in front of your face, and taking in their last breaths, all these scenarios in my life made the moment of just losing a job a little easier. There really wasn't any time for crying. It was now time to focus on picking myself off that mat because really, no one is going to do it for you.

I then said to Darcy, we're going out for a prime rib dinner tonight and celebrate me getting fired. I even watched my favorite show of Cheers that night. I went to bed thinking the next day is a new day!

When I woke up the next morning, the first thing I told Darcy was, "I'm going down to the unemployment office and after that I'm driving to the city of Orlando to walk the streets and put some resumes in." I was hoping someone might be interested in hiring me.

I started to get my unemployment checks. I continued to pound the pavement but I also took some time for myself. I started to do some things I haven't done in awhile. It was time to re-boot. I began to put some work into our new home. I did some landscaping, planting flowers, a garden, inexpensive things that didn't cost much. It was therapeutic for me and it was good to be out there by myself to think.

I started to think about the future, our kids, and how the heck I was going to pay the mortgage if I don't get a job. The first thoughts were great, but that last one had me a little worried. Especially since I was getting negative feedback from resumes I sent out telling me I was either over qualified, or the position had been filled. Needless to say, the landscaping and flower thoughts didn't last very long.

Three months went by, and I only had about three months left of unemployment checks. I said to myself, this is starting to get serious. The entire summer went by, it was two thousand four. Darcy was working full time at the school, Marissa was entering seventh grade, and the hearing aids she was wearing had no insurance benefits. The cost of her hearing aids was over four thousand dollars, out of pocket, and they were six years old. It was getting time for a new pair. I'm worrying, if they fail, what will I do? There was always complications, from molds, to batteries to cleaning them and it was getting to be that time for new ones.

Luckily, I had some money set aside for them, because if you have no hearing aids, being hearing impaired, well guess what, you're not going to hear!

We went to a place called, The Hearing Center of America, and purchased Marissa's first set of hearing aids in Florida. We had to handle this quickly because she had practice that same night. I remember it well.

The coach called the house during practice and said, "Riss is complaining that one of her hearing aids wasn't working."

"Coach, they're brand new, just bought them today. I'll come down there and get them, only thing is Coach, when she has one not working, the other one has to be taken out too. She gets dizzy when she's hearing out of only one ear, it's a balance thing."

"No problem, were just going to do some ball handling drills tonight, that's it."

When I get to the gym Marissa hands me her new hearing aids. I quickly noticed that they were wet from the sweat that was on them. I had a feeling the amplifier shorted out on them because this happened once before back in New Jersey, but these were brand new hearing aids.

I then went home and told Darcy what happened. She was real good with noticing trouble on them. She agreed, probably the amplifier had moisture in it. We then went to the Hearing Center the next day and they confirmed the same thing, it was the amplifiers. I was hoping it would be the batteries because when these amplifiers fail, it usually takes three weeks to get the hearing aids back.

After explaining to Riss what happened, she had no concerns. It meant a couple of rough weeks for her in the classroom and on the basketball court but she never complained. It was always like, no worries Dad, I got this. She was always very resilient and grateful that she was just able to hear what she could hear.

That September, I finally get a call for an interview. It was the City of Orlando Public Works Department. I was excited about it because I thought, okay, maybe this is where I begin my new career.

I spoke with the secretary and she asked me, "Mr. Cimino, we have your resume and application. Our department head was looking at it. Is it possible for you to come in tomorrow for an interview?"

My heart was racing a hundred times a minute! I told her, "Absolutely, what time?"

She replied, "Two p.m."

That night at dinner, I asked Darcy if she could pick up Riss from school and bring her to practice tomorrow. Darcy asked me why and I told her, "I have an interview!" We were both very excited.

The next day, I arrived fifteen minutes early, of course, and I was brought in at two p.m. as scheduled. The Manager asked what kind of experience I had in public works. He said, "I noticed you have been working for a newspaper all your life, why are you here?"

I told him, "A friend of mine once told me he was selling his newspaper business, and there was going to be a day where I was going to have to make a decision on a new career choice because the newspaper business was a dying industry. He said I had a lot to offer with all the experiences I had in my life and advised me that one day I should start thinking outside the box. So, I put my resume in with you, mentioning the newspaper, my experience, and all the volunteer work I did for my town back in New Jersey. I figured, maybe with my public relations experience, the City of Orlando might be the place to get a job. I read you had great benefits, great starting pay and a 401k package. It would bring stability into my life, a great atmosphere to work at, and the kind of career I might be looking for. I would be willing to start at the lowest level of city work just as long as you can guarantee me a full time position."

The manager looked at me strangely, "I read your resume, and wondered why you applied here. I did see the excellent qualifications, awards of exceptional work and a community involvement second to none. I just wanted to meet you in person."

"Does that mean I have the job?"

"Not quite. Look, Mr. Cimino, can I call you Tony?"

"Sure."

He continued, "Don't take this the wrong way, but how old are you, about forty-two, forty-three years old? I'm going to be open and honest with you. I noticed your impeccable record on your resume, I also noticed you really don't have any city or government experience other than volunteer work. You have been wrapped up in four walls for the last twenty-five years inside a newspaper pressroom. It's a different world out here right now. We're looking for younger executive types coming from college, with a Masters Degree, or someone from another professional office that offers managerial experience. I

177

noticed on your resume you didn't even attend college. Now, I know you're a little older with more knowledge and experience than those college graduates, but right now we're looking for a younger group of men and or women who we can mold into this position. Those points alone would disqualify you from this job."

"Fair enough, I can understand some of your reasoning for not giving me an opportunity, and you were very open and honest with your position and I appreciate that. However at forty-four years of age, and being told that I basically can't adapt to this position, if you don't mind me saying, it sounds like your labeling me over the hill and that I should just hang it up and call it a day! If that's what you think of me, then this is definitely not a place I would want to work at."

"Look Tony. I like you, this is Florida and you're a northerner. You're going to find out there's a lot of things different down here."

"Haven't I heard that before."

"The job market is a funny market down here and I'm sure some of it won't make any sense to you, but unfortunately, I have nothing I can offer you at this time. Good luck, it was a pleasure meeting with you."

And that was it. I walked out of the office that day thinking for the first time in my life, I was never going to get another job that I was qualified for. I started asking God questions about where He wanted me to go in my life, what His plans were, how was I going to feed my family.

I started to worry. It has been six months on unemployment and the checks were done, and no one was calling. Doctor bills that we owed since Darcy's breast cancer surgery were still due, Marissa's doctor bills from when she was young going through speech and hearing therapy were still due, and I still owed some money on her hearing aids. Needless to say, with the mortgage, food, utility bills, car payments, and only one income coming into the house, we were having a hard time making ends meet.

I went home that day feeling depressed, and burnt out. Over the course of six months, I must have submitted two hundred resumes, from the public works department, to managing a bowling alley, to working in a restaurant, and *no one* was interested in hiring me.

So here we are, a new home in Florida, no friends or family around, and no job. I get desperate. I come home and let Darcy know about the news, and she's not happy about what happened either. I said to her "Listen, what was said to me today is probably true. I have no experience other than being in a four walled building of newspaper presses over the past twenty years. What do you say I make a call back home to Jersey to Scott Erhardt. You remember him, the new Pressroom Manager at the Asbury Park Press? Maybe I can get my old job back."

Stunned, she said, "What about here? What am I supposed to do with you being up there?"

"Honey, if they hire me back, we'll make it temporary, but not tell them that, it'll help us stay afloat. If I have to travel back and forth some weekends to make it work, I'll do it."

Begrudgingly Darcy said, "Make the call."

The next day, I called Scott, the Pressroom Manager, at the Asbury Park Press in New Jersey. It just so happened, he was a pressman that I trained before I left and now he was the Pressroom Manager. I thought, if I asked him if I could get my job back there, I felt confident he would bring me back.

The call and conversation went great! He said, "Tony I can't believe you just called, you would be a valuable asset to us. We would love to have you back. We just released a pressman yesterday and one of the guys around me said, of all people we lost man, I miss Tony Cimino. And now you call! What a coincidence! Let me get you your salary back from where you left, would that be a problem?"

I told Scott, "Thank you, I just appreciate the opportunity your giving me right now."

"Hey man, you trained me. If it weren't for you, I wouldn't be in this position right now, and so many others you trained are doing great too. You were one of the best Master Color Journeyman Pressman we ever had in this building! Let me work on this, I'll get back with you first thing tomorrow."

After that phone call, I had mixed emotions. On one hand I felt relief, relief that I would have a job and be able to support my family. On the other hand, I felt anguish. Anguish on having a job but being away from my family. However, I was so grateful Scott remembered me that way, and how positive he was about bringing me back. I knew by accepting my old job, I would be leaving home and I wouldn't be going "home". But, it was survival time, and we were out of options. If flying back and forth was the way to get some money back in the house, then this was the only choice.

I told Darcy about how the phone call went and what Scott had said to me. I explained to her that at this time, I really had no choice but to go back to New Jersey so we would have money coming into the house. Reluctantly, she agreed, we had no choice.

That night, we sat down at the dinner table as a family, like we always did, and we talked about the events of the day. As parents, we always did this. Every night we would all sit down at the dinner table for about an hour and we would all talk about each other's day, and if there was anything on anyone's mind, it was time to "get it out". Good or bad you had to put it on the table.

We did this because my dad always taught me, it was better to bring your problems out on the table, than it was for him to hear it outside on the streets. The last thing I would want to hear, coming from someone else's mouth on the outside, was if my kids did something wrong to the point where it would embarrass our family. As a dad, I wanted to know everything about the behavior of my kids outside the home. I wanted them to know I was paying attention to them.

While at the dinner table, we called Michael. We told him about me going back to work in New Jersey. He was very mature about it. He said, "Dad, you always told me you have to do what you have to do to support your family. You always said there's going to be things you won't want to do, but for the greater good, for the sake of your family, and if it was the right thing to do in your mind, you have to do it."

"I said that? Maybe I should get a diploma!"

He replied, "Dad, get back to Jersey, it will work out."

It wasn't as easy for my daughter. I talked to her about it and she said, "Dad, you've been rebounding shots for me in the driveway since the fourth grade, picking me up from school, bringing me to practice, I don't want you to go!"

Then Darcy spoke up and said, "Riss, Dad, needs to work honey, those Nike basketball sneakers, uniforms, trips to camps, exposures out of State, and AAU games all cost money, besides all that, we need to put food on the table, pay for the house and other things we need in order to live. I'm not happy about this decision either, but right now, we have no choice."

Marissa was not happy. She continued, with tears in her eyes, "Dad, I want to play professional basketball someday or at least college ball and I want you to be proud of me! I want to show people no matter what, if I go completely deaf, you could set your heart on goals, dreams, and achieve them. But if you have to leave dad, I understand."

At that moment, we couldn't have been more proud of our children

The next day, I got a phone call from Scott. I was anticipating to hear from him about a starting date, salary and position. But instead, what I got was something I definitely was not prepared for, something I never even considered.

"Tony." said Scott. "I have some bad news for you. Last night there was a meeting. Personnel, Corporate, Bob Crawford, and myself. We were discussing your situation. The meeting did not go as planned. I'll just say it, Mr. Crawford was adamant about not bringing you back here. He made it very clear to us that he was never in favor of bringing any former employee back because he felt that if he was transferred, resigned, or terminated, his values were diminished because he was never committed to the company."

Then Scott told me he spoke to Mr. Crawford with disgust and said in front of everyone, "Wait! This is Tony Cimino we're talking about here, for Christ's sake! He has a damn plaque out there in the atrium!"

Mr. Crawford's reply was, "Be careful Scott, that was before my time, and with another company, make the call and let him know he's not allowed back here."

And that was it. I told Scott, "You remember that Union dispute, the way things went down? He was embarrassed about that and I believe this was his chance for revenge."

Scott said, "I'm so sorry Tony, I tried, even the guys are miffed about it. There's nothing more I can do."

"It's alright, I appreciate everything you said, and did. Tell the guys I miss them, I'll keep in touch once in awhile just to bother you."

He then said, "Tony, I love you man, thank you for everything you did for me."

After that call, my thought was how to explain this to Darcy. As soon as she came home from work, I told her everything about what had happened. She could not believe what she heard.

She then said something to me that would change our lives and to this day, I'll never forget it. It made me realize how special she was, how God speaks within us, how under the most dire of times, a simple suggestion speaks louder and clearer than anything else and yet, you have no idea how important it is, and how crazy it sounds, until one day, later on in life, you know, and you remember.

She said, "Tony, if we have to pick up a mop and bucket and go out and clean houses to make some money, that's what we're going to do!"

This suggestion has now become a mission. I felt it in my bones, and in my heart, that this was the way Our Lord was leading us to go.

Just looking back at what had happened to us, everything we have been through. We have survived, we have maintained our faith, and God has guided us and answered our prayers continuously. We have fallen on hard times and lost many family members. But we have two wonderful kids, a beautiful home and a wonderful loving marriage that has lasted for almost twenty-five years!

Darcy said, "Unpack, you're not going anywhere, we're not going anywhere. Tomorrow, we will put an ad in the paper. We will call our business *Darcy's Cleaning Service, Inc.* We will go to the Deland municipal building and file for a license, and we will incorporate our business. We can do this!"

"Your strong points are, you're great with people, your honest, intelligent and you're a hard worker. I'm good with the computer, so I can handle the office end of the business. We'll see what happens, but I feel this is the way to go."

I agreed with her, and thought it was a great idea, then again, what else could we do? So why not! Let's get that mop and go to work!

Chapter XVII
Just Say Yes

"Just say yes" that was my motto. After all the experiences I have had dealing with people, at work, with friends, community residents, parents, coaches, city council, bowling, interviewers, supervisors, advertisers, executives, police, fireman, doctors, nurses, even my wife, the one thing everyone always wants to hear is **yes**.

Yes is a positive word, with positive results, providing you don't abuse it or allow other people to abuse it. **Yes** sounds so much better than that negative word, **no**. I mean it's as simple as it sounds, isn't it? Besides, no just sounds terrible! Who gets things done with no? For example, Tommy, take the dog out. No! Dad, can I have five bucks? No! Mr. Plangere, can I have a raise? No!

But turn it around the other way by saying, Honey, can we go out to dinner tonight? Yes! Joey, did you do your homework last night? Yes! Hey, Betty, did you lose weight recently? Yes!

With our new business, I used this example. That set forth a positive attitude when a new perspective client called our service and it worked tremendously.

Our first ad in the newspaper read, *Darcy's Cleaning Service, Inc. Honest, Reliable, Hardworking, Customer Satisfaction Guaranteed, Spotlessness is Our Specialty, Twenty-five percent off first clean, Free Estimates, Please Call.*

Then I had one thousand fliers printed up at Office Depot showing the same advertisement. I stuck them on cars, put them in front doors of homes, and store front entrances. I even got permission to stand outside Dunkin Donuts and I handed them out to customers as they left.

I found a printing site called Vista print, where I had five hundred business cards printed. I took them and dropped them off to local restaurants, Laundromats, and new construction home sites, with the hope that I would get at least one call.

For the first month, no calls were coming in, but I never gave up. The more days that went by, the more fliers and business cards I handed out, and then it happened!

My first customer call came. I answered the phone, "Darcy's Cleaning Service, may I help you?"

A woman asked, "Are you new in the area? I haven't seen your business advertised in the paper before."

"Yes, as a matter of fact, we are a small family Mom and Pop business with old school standards. We work Monday through Friday and some weekends too, how can I help you?"

"I was looking for someone to clean my house every two weeks, dust, do the bathrooms, kitchen, bedrooms and I would like to know how much you charge?"

"First, I would like to come over and meet you, talk to you about your needs, wants, and your priorities. How does that sound?"

"That sounds wonderful! Do you clean windows?"

"Yes."

"Do you do blinds?"

"Yes we do."

She then hesitated and said, "My husband is handicapped and sometimes he has accidents in the shower, if you know what I mean. Would you be able to clean that up if it happened?"

My first inclination on how to respond to that was hell no! But when your back is up against the wall, and you have a motto to stick to, the only answer that is the correct one is, "**Yes**."

"God bless your heart." she replied. "Can you come over today?"

"Yes ma'am, absolutely."

That was the way my first business call went. I ended up getting the job and felt a wonderful sensation of satisfaction.

When Darcy got home for dinner I said, "Honey, great news. I landed my first client, making fifty dollars every two weeks. Only problem is, I have to clean a shower for a handicapped person. Sometimes he has accidents in the shower, if you know what I mean."

She wasn't happy about that, but understood we had to start somewhere, we had no choice.

That night after dinner, the phone rang. I answered it, "Darcy's Cleaning Service."

The gentleman on the phone asked, "Do you clean offices?"

"Yes we do."

"How much?"

"I normally don't do sight unseen estimates. If you would like, I could come by tonight and give you an estimate."

"That would be great! I appreciate your immediate attention."

He told me his name was Chip and he gave me the address of his office.

About an hour later, I met with Chip, and we agreed on cleaning his office once a week for fifty dollars. His office was to be cleaned on Friday nights. This job put our sales income now at three hundred dollars a month. Not a lot of money, but it was a start.

As the month went by, I landed a few more homes and with the combination of Darcy's job and my monthly sales, we finally had enough to pay the mortgage and put food on the table with a couple of hundred dollars to spare.

As two thousand five approached, we were still just getting by financially. It seemed that our cleaning business idea might work out, only problem was, our credit cards were starting to get maxed out.

We were paying doctor bills with them, getting new work clothes, and putting the cleaning business expenses on our charge cards. We were charging vacuums, rags, cleaning products, supplies and any miscellaneous items that we needed to run our business. Our credit was deteriorating and it was getting difficult to pay for other things that were needed.

Marissa's basketball expenses were taking its toll on us too. Uniforms, sneakers, sports bra's, AAU expenses, and traveling to all the gyms where she played were costly.

If things weren't bad enough in our budget, one more call made it even worse.

Our son Michael called us one night and said, "Mom, Dad, I have a problem. It's my junior year and I start my teaching internship in Delaware County. The professor said it's a mandatory rule that students are responsible for their own transportation to the schools where they are training. Is it possible you can lend me some money to buy a second hand car?"

That was the last thing we wanted to hear, but I wasn't going to dare tell him about our financial problems.

I told Michael, "Let me work on that, can I get back with you tomorrow?"

"Sure Dad, one other thing, I made the Dean's list again last semester."

"Michael that's great! Man, your kicking butt there aren't you?"

"Dad, I'm top five in my class of over five hundred teachers!"

"Congratulations Michael, let me talk to Mom about this. I'll call you tomorrow and let you know what we came up with."

After getting off the phone with him, I was so proud, but so upset with myself. Here I am just getting by with the monthly bills, and I'm having thoughts of telling him we're broke and I can't help him. But I couldn't do that, I just had to find a way.

I went to Darcy and explained the situation, and we both agreed that our son is the most important person right now, and he needs to finish college. She came up with the idea to offer him our nineteen ninety-six Jeep Grand Cherokee. We could give it to him when he comes down for Christmas. As for us, we can both use our other car, a 2003 Hyundai, to get back and forth, until he graduates.

I called Michael and told him the news, and he was ecstatic. I said, "Listen son, this is a temporary solution for now until you graduate. When you get home we need the car back."

He couldn't thank us enough. He promised us he would take care of the car and promised to finish on the University of Delaware's Deans List for the fourth time in four years. I told him we were very proud of him and to make sure he gets that diploma.

Going into the summer of two thousand five, all those business cards, fliers and advertisements in the newspaper were finally starting to pay off. I had about ten houses to clean which was making us almost seven hundred dollars a month. Then, Darcy's job at All Souls Catholic School called to renew her position as a school aide. Finances started to get a little better.

Back in New Jersey, our son Michael, was on summer break from school and decided he wanted to stay there. He told me he landed a job at BJ's Wholesale store and he met up with an old friend of mine, Joe Tomaino. He asked me if it was okay with me for him to spend the summer at Joe's. Joe had a finished basement and would only charge Michael three hundred dollars a month to stay.

"Honestly Michael, I would prefer if you came back here and stayed with us. You can get a job here, save some money and be ready for your last year in Delaware."

Michael then asked, "Dad, you raised me to work right? To be responsible, and make grown up decisions for myself. If you don't mind, I'd rather stay here, things would be easier for me."

I hesitantly agreed. It was probably the right decision for everyone. At that time, Marissa was playing at a higher level of AAU basketball on a state sanctioned team called DEBO (Defensive Energy Brings Offense) and the finances to stay and play on the team were very costly.

DEBO was a traveling team that played all over the state of Florida and sometimes would go to North Carolina and Duke University to play in competitive competitions against teams from all over the country and I knew this was going to be expensive.

This is what parents do right, we make decisions based on the goals we set as parents to give our children the best opportunity for them to succeed. Most importantly, they both loved what they were doing. As long as they were willing to work, put the time in and be dedicated, we knew we had to at least meet them halfway.

A week later, after solving all those issues, I had a great business breakthrough. I received a telephone call from Lynelle, who represented St. Joe Builders. She was inquiring about construction cleaning. She asked if I would be willing to come down to her office to meet with her and discuss the possibility of a construction cleaning job. I immediately told her, "Yes I would. When would you like to meet?"

She asked, "How does two p.m. sound?"

I told her I would be looking forward to it.

When I arrived, she explained that she represented St. Joe Builders Association and she was responsible for the completion of a retirement community, Victoria Park. She went on to say, "We would like your company to clean our new construction homes after our contractor's work is completed. I can't guarantee how many homes I would have every week for you to clean, however, I can offer to pay you two hundred thirty-seven dollars and fifty cents for every home I assign to you."

Very excited, I told her, "That would be fantastic, I'll take the job!"

My thoughts were, this was a major account to add to my portfolio, and the positive feedback could lead to more jobs. I took this as an excellent opportunity to establish our future as a company. With Darcy working full time and this new opportunity, we both thought maybe this could change our financial burdens in a more positive direction. The business was almost earning one thousand dollars a month and I felt confident more opportunities were on the horizon. And I was right!

I then received another telephone call. This time it was from a preschool called Christian Care for Little Angels. Their job required me to work during the summer from the hours of three p.m. to six p.m. The job consisted of cleaning lunch tables, vacuum, take the trash out and mop the floors. I asked the manager Tracy, "What is the school offering for this position?"

She said, "How about ten dollars an hour, six hundred dollars a month?"

I told her, "Yes. I'll take the job."

On my way home, after I committed to that job, my thoughts were, this was not a house to clean, it was a school and what better way to earn money without having to do master bathrooms. Now we were up to sixteen hundred dollars a month, and surviving a little better.

For my business, jobs kept coming in. Plus, over the summer, Darcy got a part-time job with the Deltona

Recreation program working from June through September. You would think with all this positive news, life financially would be getting better. But no matter how much we tried, those awful credit card minimum payments were approaching more than one hundred seventy-five dollars a month and there were about five of them. We continued to keep our head up, trying to stay positive, and always made sure the kids didn't know about our financial problems.

At the start of the next school year, Marissa was entering eighth grade and Michael was entering his senior year at Delaware. We reassured him over the summer he could continue to use our Jeep Grand Cherokee to finish his internship program.

At Deltona Middle school, we had another IEP meeting and it basically went over all the goals that were set forth for Marissa so she could be successful in the classroom.

In her basketball life, the middle school was running a recreation basketball league, and there was a notice for sign ups near the gym. It didn't say anything about being a boys league or a girls league. So the girls on her AAU team had a meeting and said to each other why don't we sign up as a team, we're in the eighth grade, were pretty good, let's play. Come to find out, they were the only girls team to sign up for that recreational league.

That night, I get a phone call from Coach Palmer. Coach Palmer said to me, "Tony, my daughter Paige came home and said there was a big commotion in school about our girls playing in a recreation league with the boys. I called the school up, talked to the principal and he told me they could play under one condition. The principal told me I couldn't coach the team because I was already coaching the high school girls team, so what do you say?"

"Are you asking me to coach the girls team?"

"Yes you could do it, just let them run the plays I taught them in practice, it will be fine. All the girls know the color language plays, Marissa will play point guard, and she'll call the plays."

"Coach, all these teams are full of eighth grade boys, right?"

"Our girls are competitive, besides it will be a good challenge for them before I get them next year."

In the first two games, they were surprisingly playing pretty good, losing by ten points and twelve points respectfully. Then the craziest thing happened.

On the third game, the gym was packed because they had three games. One was a makeup game because it rained like a monsoon the week before and they canceled all the games. So there were double the amount of parents and spectators in the gym that night.

We ended up playing this boys team that only had one loss. By half time, the score was fifteen to twelve, in our favor. Marissa was having a great game, and so was her teammate, Jessenia.

The crowd even took notice and was getting very vocal and excited about how the game was being played against the boys and they were anticipating a girls win.

In the fourth quarter of the game, with two minutes left, the score was tied twenty-three, twenty-three and the gym was loud and noisy as ever. It was a packed house, standing room only crowd.

Marissa, playing point guard, runs a play, passes, gets the ball back and dribbles to the basket and gets fouled. She makes her two free throws making the score twenty-five, twenty-three, the girls are winning!

The boy's coach then calls time out and we hear him screaming at his team, saying, "You guys want to get beat by a bunch of girls?"

Marissa turns to me and said, "Dad, his voice is so loud, even I can hear him, plus the gym is so loud, would you mind holding onto my hearing aids?"

I took her hearing aids and told the team, "Go out there and play, have fun and enjoy the moment."

As time was running down, another boys missed shot and another two point basket by Jessenia clinches the game!

For the next few days, it was the talk around the school, it was a defining moment and game for Marissa and the whole team.

Marissa came up to me after the game and said "Dad, hearing or not, you think I'm pretty good, don't you?"

"You played fantastic tonight. I'm so proud of you."

I then called Coach Palmer and he said, "Everyone heard about the game, man! This town is anticipating some special things from these girls, congrats on the win."

We finished the season out in November, and it was the only time they beat a boys team that year, but that was an accomplishment they'll never forget.

In November, high school basketball season was starting up and Marissa's AAU basketball team was back playing. I remember one tournament in November, Darcy wasn't feeling too good. She told me, "At work the other day, I had a bad coughing attack and I think I hurt my rib."

As time went on, the pain was getting worse. Finally, during Christmas break, Darcy decided to go get checked out by the doctor.

Darcy underwent many x-rays and blood work. About a week later, we received the phone call we hoped we would never receive again. Darcy's doctor called and wanted her to come into the office for all her test results. Darcy insisted she be told over the phone and hesitantly her doctor told her she possibly had lung cancer and had to undergo a biopsy. Darcy insisted to her doctor that she felt it was only her ribs but her doctor had her go to see a surgeon anyway.

I immediately called Darcy's oncologist from New Jersey, Dr. Susan Greenberg. I explained to Dr. Greenberg what was going on and Dr. Greenberg reminded me of what she told both of us years ago. Dr. Greenberg said, "Because of the high dose of chemotherapy Darcy received, her bones would become fragile and weak and it was important for Darcy to take high quantities of calcium. So it would be possible for her to fracture or break her ribs."

After getting off the phone with Dr. Greenberg I felt better, but Darcy's current oncologist still had her scheduled for the biopsy.

Darcy had the biopsy done in January at Central Florida Regional Hospital, and we were told it would take up to two weeks to get the results.

I asked her, "Do you want to tell the kids?"

"No." she said. "Riss has an AAU basketball tournament next week. The last thing I want to do is let her know and Michael has mid terms. I don't want to disrupt his agenda either, he's been very focused and working hard. Let's see where this is going."

After a tough work week and thinking the worst, because that's what you always do when you hear news like this, we decided to put it in God's hands, pray for the best and went to the University of Florida to enjoy ourselves and watch Riss play basketball.

The Friday before the tournament, like always, we packed several bags of miscellaneous needs for a weekend tournament. Extra sports bras, sneakers, sweatbands, and Gatorade. It's amazing how many items a ballplayer needs to perform!

Still waiting for the surgeon to call, praying for good news, we leave for Gainesville. Finally, halfway to Gainesville, Darcy receives a phone call from her surgeon.

I look over at her and she has her hand over her mouth. Then, I see tears coming down her face. I pulled over thinking the worse. Her cancer is back.

Darcy hangs up, turns to me and said, "Oh my God, you're not going to believe this. They said it was a false reading, the only thing wrong with me is what I told them, I have two broken ribs!"

"Alleluia!"

Needless to say, I was completely relieved. However, I was disgusted that they had to stick a tube down her throat and put her through numerous other tests plus stress us out for over three weeks.

We were all so relieved we were actually able to enjoy the campus, the games, and the atmosphere for the entire weekend.

After several games and great play by our daughter, the weekend was a success. Marissa ended up having one of her best tournaments.

As a matter of fact, at one of the games, the University of Florida woman's basketball coach was in attendance and Riss hit a game winning shot in front of her! After the game she came over to congratulate Riss and asked, "What high school are you attending?"

Riss replied, "Pine Ridge Coach."

Coach Baxter then told her, "Well if you keep hitting shots like that, you could be playing for us in this gym one day," and then she walked away.

We were so proud of her.

On the way home we were all saying the weekend's festivities made all those worrisome nights a distant memory. Knowing Darcy's cancer was gone and our daughter's future was going as planned, things were looking up.

We then called our son Michael in Delaware and told him the news about everything that had happened. His

196

reply was, "One day you guys should write a book about all you have been through. Maybe someone who has cancer and is fighting it might feel a little better reading about your story knowing that there is hope out there. Maybe one day Mom and Dad, they'll find a cure."

Looking back at what he said, I felt the need to write this story.

Chapter XVIII
Building A Business

As we were entering two thousand six, our business started to generate a multitude of clients who wanted their homes cleaned. I decided to put a help wanted ad in the local newspaper for the first time. The advertisement read as follows: *Housecleaner needed, must be reliable, honest, responsible, and must have their own transportation, fifteen to twenty hours a week. Starting pay is eight dollars an hour with bonuses and incentives.*

This was the first time in my life I was on the other side of business conducting interviews for an employee I needed. I went to Office Depot and designed my own application for Darcy's Cleaning Service, Inc. It was a basic application I copied off a standard formatted one. The usual information such as; former employers, references, social security number, etc.

Then I designed my own brochures. I included pictures of people's homes that I cleaned, the cost of services, and what our company offered.

The only thing I wasn't prepared for was the bombardment of phone calls I was going to get from people who wanted a job. I remember there were tough times and hardships back then.

Two thousand six and two thousand seven had a government financial crisis happening. The housing market was at an all time low, construction was slow, electricians were out of work, plumbers, landscapers, even house painters were out of jobs. There was no work for anyone.

I started to remember all those months I was walking the streets looking for a job, thinking about these people calling me for a job. But I needed to stay focused on one thing that was vitally important, this was **my** company, and they were going to work for me. Which meant they were going to represent my business, my reputation, and my standards. There had to be guidelines set in place on what I wanted and what I expected from them.

I also wanted to be a boss that could understand people too. That was very important to me, for one very good reason, Mr. Plangere, the owner of the Asbury Park Press, who taught me how to be a businessman. He was always very professional, and made it clear on what he expected from his workers. But he also made his employees know he wanted to be a regular kind of guy. Someone who understood hardships, financial pain and suffering.

He presently has a foundation called The Plangere Foundation in Boca Raton Florida. It is a charitable organization that gives to children in need. His generosity was something everyone knew about. So when it came time for Christmas, he didn't disappoint his employees. Christmas bonuses every year and turkeys for the families on Thanksgiving were the norm. A real family man who wanted to treat his employees like family. It was important for him to show his employees he wasn't just a businessman, but a real person too.

Mentoring him, I went into this venture thinking about how to run my business, and model it after him.

Immediately, I wanted to implement three core values. Hard work ethics, responsibility and generosity to my employees. My responsibility was to choose the right people to represent my business. I had to remember, this wasn't a newspaper, it was a housecleaning business, and I had to alter my thinking. I'm probably not going to get people with a college degree, but more inclined to interview people who have children and need part time work to earn extra money for their families.

Another thing I had to be very careful of was not to hire a person with a criminal record. That could destroy my business. The last thing I needed was to employ a person who had committed a crime, so a background check was a must!

My first few interviews went well, and I chose to hire a young woman in her twenties. She had two kids in school, and needed a job to support them. She had been working as a waitress, and had no experience in cleaning homes.

I remember she wanted to clean homes in the mornings and wanted to be done in time to pick her kids up from school. This way she would have time to go home and make dinner, giving her enough time to get to her second job. She had a great personality, highly motivated and didn't mind working. I then asked her if she ever had any trouble with the law, convictions, traffic violations, that sort of thing. She told me she did not.

I then did my first criminal background check and there were no blemishes on her record. It seemed like she was a great person to choose for the job. I hired her immediately and felt good about growing the company to another level.

My first plan of action was to implement a time card honor system for employees to write down their hours that they worked at each house. To this day, I still use it.

The time card method shows my client's names on it. Each time the employee arrives at a house they're cleaning, they write down the time they arrived to work and the time they departed from the home.

At the end of the week, I would pick up the time card, replenish supplies needed, and pay them for the prior week worked. Pretty simple task, and it was working extremely great!

About two months into the job with this first employee I hired was when things started to get interesting.

I started to get phone calls from a couple of clients saying, "Tony, Linda your employee arrived on time at eight thirty, however, she was gone by ten thirty. Does it normally only take two hours to clean a home?"

I then asked the client, "How long has this been happening?"

She told me the last two cleans. I asked, "Can you please do me a favor? Next clean, let me know what time she gets there and call me when she's finished. I want to know because her time card indicates she's been at your house for three hours."

The next time Linda was scheduled to clean, the client called me as promised and said, "Tony, Linda showed up on time today, but I just left the beach in Daytona which is about fifteen minutes from my house, and you're not going to believe this, but I think I just saw her walking on the boardwalk. It's ten thirty, shouldn't she be at my house cleaning?"

I thanked the client for calling me and assured her I would check into this situation. I compensated her for the clean and promised her by her next clean, the problem would be solved.

After I got off the phone with my client, I took a drive to the beach to see if I could spot Linda, my employee. I was only about fifteen minutes away.

Upon arriving at the beach, I see Linda's car parked on the street with the parking meter indicating she had been there a half hour. Then I see her sunbathing on the beach! I approached her and asked, "Linda, what time did you get done at Mrs. Jones' house?"

She replied, "Ten minutes ago."

"Okay, that means you cleaned the house in an hour and forty-five minutes?"

Not even looking at me, she replied, "Yes."

I then asked her, "How many times have you left the house early to come down here?"

Her response was, "If you don't get away from me now, I'll call the cops and file harassment charges against you."

"Linda, then just go get my supplies out of your car and I'll be on my way."

"Get them yourself."

I realized this conversation was going nowhere, so I left the beach area where she was laying at, went up to the boardwalk and approached a police officer.

After explaining my volatile situation, the officer said to me, "Wait here. I'll get her to open her car up so you can get your supplies."

I then witnessed both of them in a highly contested confrontation down on the beach where she was sunbathing. After five minutes of yelling at the officer, he was finally able to get Linda back to her car.

As she opens the trunk, she starts to throw all of my liquid supplies out into the street. My vacuum, the mop and bucket are thrown next. Now I'm thinking, what did I hire, a crazed woman? The officer got a chuckle out of it. But I was embarrassed.

I learned a valuable lesson that day. The next time I hire someone, call the references, don't take anything for granted.

When I returned home, I wanted to look at her application again t see if maybe I missed something. I took it upon myself to call a couple of her former jobs, and friends, which I should have done in the first place.

After speaking with a couple of her former bosses, I learned Linda had a bad temper, which cost her two jobs before mine. Live and learn.

Chapter XIX
Reality

That day I learned to become my own Human Resource Manager and vowed to do a better job on the application process next time.

When Darcy got home from work, I was all ready to tell her about what happened, but it seemed she had something else on her mind. I asked her, "Are you okay?"

She said, "Not really."

"Are you sick?"

With tears in her eyes, she said, "No."

I then asked her, "What's going on? Come on we can fix it, we always do."

She then started to get emotional. She started raising her voice at me in anger. "Look at me!" she yelled. "I have no boobs, clothes that don't fit me anymore, my prosthesis are no longer supportive in my bras because my bras are stretched and old, I don't feel like a woman anymore, want to hear some more?" Then she started to cry.

Now, I'm here thinking I'm going to tell her about my day? That's not happening. So, I said to her, "Listen honey, we will fix this. We will find a breast cancer clothing shop, there's got to be one around. We'll go get some new clothes, we'll get some new bras, and we'll get you feeling better."

The conversation was just a reminder of how fortunate I was to still have her here and living. It was also a reminder of what she had to go through every day physically, mentally and emotionally to get prepared just to go out. It was something I really never thought about.

One thing about Darcy though, she never complained about her condition after the operation. She never had a feel sorry for me attitude. She would get up every morning like clockwork. She would go through the motions, take a shower, get dressed, and get her day going.

To this day, the prosthesis has to be washed every night, placed in a box to keep its shape, so it's always ready to be placed in the bra the next morning.

Only today, this outburst opened my eyes. I guess as a man, a husband, a father, I was just so focused on getting the job done. You know work, come home, play with the kids, give your wife what she needs. Hugs, chores, cut the lawn, help her clean around the house, take her out to dinner once in awhile, you know, usual stuff.

She lead me to believe, she was alright. But inside she was hurting, not because she had no breasts, but because she didn't feel normal. All she wanted was some clothes to fit her, ones that don't have a V-neck where the shirt comes down her neck close to showing her scars from the surgery. Or having to buy a two piece bikini. That wasn't happening anymore, but that was okay for her. She just needed to start feeling good about herself again. She was in a funk, and I needed to help her.

The regular stores just weren't satisfying her anymore. She would find a great one piece bathing suit at the mall and that would be great, but it was the strapless dresses that couldn't be worn by her anymore that really started to bother her.

Looking back, I guess I was just so happy she didn't die, like her other two sisters so this problem just wasn't important to me. It was like, look honey, your living! And I'm a lucky guy too!

But I found out that day it wasn't just about living, it was about living a happy life, a quality life, one that you can feel good about.

Now that doesn't mean Darcy wasn't happy, it just meant she wanted to get some of her self esteem back. The hard times and days that we experienced were just going by without a thought. Now was the time for her to start getting back her motivation to live, to make her feel good about her body again. Maybe getting her back to working out and running on a daily basis.

For the next few weeks we started focusing on her. Making her feel good again, look better in clothes that fit. We would visit some different stores that had catered to breast cancer survivors. That wasn't an easy task because there weren't many stores like that around.

Then one day, we found a great store in Daytona Beach called Heart Strings. It was a store that catered towards breast cancer victims. As we walked into the store, we knew this was the right place to be. The staff must of seen the look in Darcy's eyes. They were so friendly and knew exactly what she was going through, and what she wanted. This store had specially made bathing suits, tank tops and all kinds of bras, even several new prosthesis.

Going back and thinking about the day when I terminated my worker, and picked my vacuum up off the street, that day started off so bad, but turned out to be one of the most humbling days of my life.

When we finally got home after shopping, and I mean *finally*, I was able to explain to Darcy what had happened to the employee I hired. Darcy was pretty positive about it, and said, "Well, we both learned a lesson today. I guess this cleaning business requires a certain person to hire and we have to be more diligent with the process. It seems to me you might have to hire a more mature woman, who resembles our work ethic, more conscientious, maybe a little older with no little kids to worry about. Maybe people who have kids in high school and need to fill their day to make a little extra money for themselves. As much as you want to give a younger person a chance, the job calls for someone who has the least amount of responsibilities to tend to at home. An older person really might be the way to go."

I took her advice and hired a middle aged woman the next day. Her name was Lisa. Her kids were in high school, and she was looking for extra money to have in her pocket for spending. I checked out all of her references, and they gave her great reviews. Background check had no blemishes on it, and her former employer gave her a great recommendation. So I hired her. She turned out to be wonderful. I was so thrilled. I had chosen a great employee to help me clean my homes.

I really needed to do this, because my business was growing and starting to multiply. The most important thing was she had experience and a really good attitude.

Going into April that year, our son Michael graduated from the University of Delaware with Honors and made a decision to move to Florida. We couldn't be happier! He immediately applied to the Volusia County school system. It only took a week for him to be hired as a Science teacher. We were so proud of him.

The next thing on his agenda was to have his girlfriend Caryn move down here with him. He told us, "I know it's kind of sudden, but I just want to let you both know, I plan on marrying her someday."

I asked Michael, "Do you have any plans to get an apartment?"

Michael's reply was, "If you don't mind, can we both stay at home here, for a few weeks? We have an apartment complex I already checked out, and we just need some time to get things settled."

My first thought was, hell no, but my response was, "Okay sure, only for a few weeks."

Caryn was a sweet girl, was in love with our son, and she asked me if I could help her find a job. We felt obligated to help, it was the least we could do for both of them knowing they wanted to move down to Florida to be with family.

Darcy and I both agreed on this decision because of all the family losses we sustained, this was a welcoming event, a loving decision. It was great to have our son back home and it was great to see both of our kids together again in the same house, even if it was just for a little while.

Around the same time it just so happened Marissa was finishing out middle school and getting ready for high school, with major anticipation and aspirations of a wonderful basketball career.

Our thoughts were our family was healthy, school was good, our son was home and figuring out his future and most of all Darcy was feeling pretty good about herself again.

Now, it was time to get back to work, with a new employee and start building that business. However, before that could happen, there was one persistent problem that wouldn't go away.

Our financial debt was coming to a head, and the financial problems were something we just couldn't overcome.

Chapter XX
Bankruptcy

Our credit cards finally ruined us financially. We exhausted all efforts trying to accommodate the credit counselors, we even asked them to lower our payments so we could afford to pay them. Instead, they raised our minimum payment on each card from one hundred seventy-five dollars to over three hundred dollars a month. At that amount, they became impossible to pay. It was now to the point a bankruptcy lawyer was needed.

Not really knowing any attorneys in the area, and being too ashamed to ask anyone for a reference, we looked in our community newspaper and found a lawyer that had an office about fifteen minutes from our home.

At our first appointment with Gina Sanchez, our bankruptcy attorney, she had us bring in all of our credit card statements, our house deed, car titles, students loan papers that we co-signed for our son Michael, and all of our doctor bills.

Darcy and I both were sick to our stomach over this meeting because we never asked anyone for financial help. We even paid for our own wedding. This was a very difficult time for us to go through. But again, we really had no choice, there was no family around that could help us.

During the summer, we started seeing Gina on a regular basis. She had a plan on how to payback creditors without feeling the crunch with our own living expenses. Easier said than done and I'm sure anyone who's been through a bankruptcy will be able to relate to this. The big question for us was, how do you live within your means financially, without being able to buy the things you need the most?

We had a cleaning business to tend to and it needed supplies and products. Vacuums cost about one hundred fifty dollars each, and when you're cleaning houses every day, the wear and tear on them make their shelf life short.

Our attorney organized a fantastic plan with our debtors and she was placing us into chapter thirteen bankruptcy. The idea was to get our major debts discharged with a minimum monthly payback installment, for three years, that would satisfy our creditors.

Credit cards like Visa, MasterCard, Macys and Home Depot would take lower monthly payments. Our parent/student loan would be negotiated to pay at a later date, even our car loan balance would be discharged because of depreciation. All in all, there would be a monthly reduction amount of almost seven hundred dollars.

I asked Gina, "Will this payback plan be approved?"

She told us, "We're going to put this plan in front of a judge and have him rule on it, more than likely he will approve it." She went on to say, "Many people are having financial problems because our economy is in financial disarray. Based on your case, with your medical and health issues, I'm sure he will show mercy on you both, but we'll have to wait and see."

After hearing that, I really didn't feel to confident about what she was explaining.

The following week was our meeting in front of the judge. I remember this day so clearly, because I was so nervous! At the time, the Bankruptcy Court was temporarily being held in downtown Orlando in the Fairwinds Building.

As we entered the building, we were directed to a room that resembled a school classroom. It was full of student desks and full of a lot of people in the same position as us.

One by one, the court clerk calls out names, then you and your attorney are escorted to the judge who will hear your case. Prior to our meeting with the judge, we could hear people at the stand saying, "Excuse me Judge, are we able to keep our houseboat?" Or, "I would like to keep our vacation home."

This completely amazed Darcy and I. Here we are, just wanting to lower our credit card monthly payments and these people want to keep boats and second homes! We were thinking, we really don't own anything, what could the judge possibly take from us?

Moments later, a few more people went in front of him and presented their case, and no mercy was given. Finally, the court clerk calls, "Mr. & Mrs. Cimino, approach the bench."

We slowly walk to the bench, we were so nervous, we didn't know what to expect. We were the type of people that would get nervous over a parking ticket, and now we're asking a judge to forgive thousands of dollars we couldn't pay back to people we owe.

It was time to sit down in front of him. Gina, our lawyer turns to me before we start and whispers in my ear, "Just relax, I have everything under control."

The Judge then starts by saying, "Mr. & Mrs. Cimino, I would like to ask, how you are both feeling today?"

I replied, in a joking manner, "Well Judge, I'm a little nervous today, especially after hearing your verdict on the last two people up here."

He started to laugh, and I'm thinking okay, he sees I have a sense of humor, I broke the ice. Then he said, "I looked at your file and I see you kids have been through some rough health issues. How are you feeling Mrs. Cimino?"

In a very quiet, nervous voice, Darcy said, "Fine Judge."

Then he asked about Marissa. He wanted to know how deaf Marissa was, and the last time she got hearing aids. Continuing, he said, "I'm concerned for her, just look at me, I'm wearing mine now too."

Darcy then said, "As for our daughter, she's amazing and she handles her disability well."

The judge then said to us, "All these people in this room approach my bench, and ask me for mercy. They want me to grant them cars, boats and houses without paying back what they owe. Here you two just want to be healthy, get the medical treatment you deserve, and help your daughter. This is the easiest case I had all day. Bankruptcy approved. On a personal note, Mr. and Mrs. Cimino, I admire both of you, and I hope my decision gives you both a little less stress in your lives and more comfort knowing you will be able to afford your daughter's needs. The court clerk will now take you and your attorney into the next room to assign you a Trustee. For the next thirty-six months, you will pay her a monthly payment of approximately three hundred eighty dollars. But I must make one thing very clear to the both of you. Miss one payment to your trustee and you will be responsible for the entire amount of the debts you owe in full, are we clear on what I just said?"

We both nodded our heads yes, and walked out of the courtroom that day paying less than a quarter of what we were paying our debtors each month.

In the hallway after the judge's decision, we were still shaking, but we were able to sigh a breath of relief. We couldn't thank Gina enough. Our feeling was maybe now we can finally get our financial life back to normal.

The first thing on our agenda was to make a strict financial budget for our house expenses, living expenses, business expenses, and medical needs.

We made a line item list of the important needs for the family such as: new hearing aids, batteries, molds, and updated hearing tests for Marissa. As for Darcy, we had a plan so we would be able to afford her new prosthesis.

Then we drew out a line item list on a spreadsheet for our business expenses. Items such as vacuum cleaners, which were the most expensive item that needed to be replaced, gas allowance, travel expenses, insurance, advertising, work clothes, cleaning products, clerical, business cards, brochures, licensing, taxes, and all other miscellaneous expenses.

It was a complete budget like we never had done before. Once that was all finished, we set aside that three hundred eighty dollars for the bankruptcy trustee.

This debt restructure plan was prioritized for three long years. We were determined to make it work. It was a plan to maintain our business, help our daughter, and get our life back to normalcy again.

That day in court, in front of that judge reassured my faith in people, the judicial system of our country and how God still provides in the most desperate times of our lives. No matter how difficult the adversity in life, it is ultimately your faith that makes you both humble and successful.

Chapter XXI
Rebuilding

As we were paying our payments to the bankruptcy trustee, we started to focus on rebuilding, not just our lives, but the lives of our children who also sacrificed for the greater good of our family.

As for Marissa, she was entering Pine Ridge High School as a freshman. First on the agenda was to schedule an appointment with the school guidance counselor, Marissa's teachers and a hearing aid advocate to go over the new IEP standards set for her high school career so she could be successful in her subjects.

In our IEP meeting we discussed using the same phonic ear system that was so beneficial for Marissa in middle school. We also implemented a note taker for Marissa. Her advocate made a good point at our meeting, that it was very hard for a hearing impaired person to listen and take notes at the same time. With a note taker, Marissa could focus on listening to the teacher and her classmates during a lecture or discussion.

After the meeting, we felt very confident with our decision, not only with Marissa playing basketball at Pine Ridge, but how the high school administration and teachers took the initiative to make her education a top priority.

We then went to visit the high school gym to see Coach Palmer. He was delighted to see us. Coach Palmer told us he couldn't wait for the season to get started. He already had Marissa penciled in as the starting point guard with two seniors and two juniors. It was the first time in Pine Ridge High School history, that a freshman was a starting player on the girls varsity basketball team.

Our son Michael and his fiancé Caryn found an apartment. It was about ten miles from our home and close to both of their jobs.

Darcy was back at All Souls, and things were going well for her there.

Now it was time to concentrate on our business goals. The idea was to build the infrastructure of the company while maintaining good business practices. My idea was to have our two employees train our new employees, and it worked out great.

The first couple of weeks, I scheduled all of them to work in pairs with the same clients. I had two reasons for that, one was for our existing employees to introduce our new employees to all of our clients. This was to build relationships. That way our clients would feel comfortable and familiar with both employees. If one called out sick, the clients would be familiar with the other. With that came trust, reliability, and responsibility.

The second reason was, once the clients became familiar with both employees, I was then able to split them up and have them individually clean homes on their own. Making more time to build the business and to be able to service more homes in the future.

During this time I was also busy cleaning homes myself. I wanted my employees to see that I was out there in the field cleaning houses too. I didn't want them to think I was one of those bosses that just show up to pay them, or to check up on them. That was important to me.

When I started this business, it was only me cleaning all the homes, so I knew how demanding and physical this job was. I realize it's not rocket science, but a good hard labor job that should be paid accordingly. With that in mind, I started hiring more employees.

I then wanted to implement a Christmas bonus plan. To me that was must. Not to bring up Mr. Plangere again, but he was such an important, vital, mentor in my life and I took his words and business advice very seriously. I basically picked his brain throughout all those years I worked for him and I was always trying to find ways in my business to emulate his concepts and ideas. The one thing I always remembered was how much a Christmas bonus improved morale.

Every year around September you would hear employees saying, two more months and we get our bonus! It's something that always made an impression on me.

So when I started interviewing people, one of the things I mentioned to them was, we give out a Christmas bonus. During the interview process, that would always get the attention of the applicant that I was interviewing. I knew immediately from their reaction how much they enjoyed hearing that incentive, and that was so important to me.

With the business being established, the bankruptcy plan working, and Darcy being healthy, it was again time to focus on Marissa. Being a high school student athlete once myself, we stressed to Marissa the importance of practice and maintaining good grades. I knew this would be a challenge because it was high school where there were new influences, different surroundings, and additional concerns.

As her dad, I was always there for her and at this time of her life, it was no different. I felt my responsibility was not only to let my kids know I was paying attention to them, but to let other kids know I was aware of them too. Now you may ask, what other kids I am talking about, high school boys of course. Dads know what I mean on that one.

In my opinion, I was sending a gorgeous brunette out on a basketball court. She is talented, and has the ability to beat any freshman boy in a game of one on one. What do you think was going to happen? That's right, a phone ringing off the wall at home with potential boyfriend prospects. Especially, other athletes who knew my daughter from the basketball court.

Without being over protective, which was very hard to do, I had to come up with a mature idea, without showing her my distrust. The last thing I wanted was to have some guy come along, take my daughter's focus away from her studies and her basketball career.

So, I brilliantly focused on two things, and two things only. On a wing and a prayer, I called Coach Palmer one night and asked him, "Do you remember when you asked me for a favor? Remember, for me to coach the eighth grade girls recreation team?"

Hesitantly he replied, "Yes."

"Well, I need to call in my marker."

"Okay, what's up?" asked Coach Palmer.

"Since my daughter has been attending high school, I really don't get to see her much anymore. She wakes up, goes to school, and heads to your practice. Then, after practice, mom brings her to speech therapy and then I go clean my offices."

"Okay, what do you want from me?"

"Would you mind if I attended a few practices with you? Maybe help you out on the court?" He was very agreeable with the idea.

So without him knowing my plan, I just synchronized my first stage of letting everyone know that Marissa's dad is out there coaching the girls team. The second part was a little more tricky, but fair minded.

After practice one night I approached Riss, and asked her a question point blank. "Be honest and upfront with me."

"Sure, Dad what's up?"

"Has there been any boys who have shown any interest in you lately? You know, in this new high school?"

She started to laugh at me saying, "Dad, this has been going on since the seventh grade, where you been?"

"Oh boy, we need to talk."

"Why what's wrong?" she asked, in a tone like I didn't trust her.

"Riss, let me make you aware of something. I'm a guy, I was in high school once too. I want to have a talk with you, maybe at dinner tomorrow with mom."

"Okay, just a talk, right?"

"Yes, that's it, just a talk."

At dinner, the following night, I didn't tell Darcy my thoughts, but I put it out on the table like we always did. I turned to Riss, and said, "Riss, I love you, second I trust you, third, I don't trust boys! Hear me out on this issue please, I'm a little worried about the boy thing, I'm a dad, so I'm allowed." I then told her, "I've come up with an idea and I want to propose a deal to you." While Darcy's sitting there listening, I said to Riss, "You're a beautiful girl, intelligent, an athlete. You are going to have many offers from boys to date in high school. I want you to know, you can go out with anyone you choose to go out with, and I do mean anyone. I will respect your choice and decision. However, there are three things I want from that boy and if I don't get those three things he's done, agreed?"

Skeptically, she looked at me and said, "It depends, what's the three things?"

Now, Darcy starts laughing, and says, "I've got to hear this!"

"Okay, first thing is easy. When picking you up for a date, he must come into the house and respect your parents by shaking my hand saying hi, Mr. and Mrs. Cimino."

"Okay." Marissa said. "What's the second thing?"

"When I ask where you guys are going, he better tell the truth."

"Okay, what's the third thing?"

"When I ask what time you're going to be home, you guys better be five minutes early from the time you both told me. That's it, and if anyone of these ground rules are broken, Mom and I have the right to lay down a punishment according to what your mother and I think is appropriate."

After intently listening, Darcy said, "That's a good deal Riss, take it." Once Darcy said that, I knew I was home free, and of course, Marissa agreed to it.

Once that problem was solved, we attended her first high school game against New Smyrna Beach. The night was exciting, Darcy and I were anticipating a great game from her. As play started we both immediately noticed the difference in the size of the players. As a freshman, Marissa was now going up against players that were bigger, quicker, older and stronger than her. But that didn't seem to make a difference. I felt confident she was ready to play against them. After all, she always played against older, more mature players all of her life, this shouldn't be any different.

She didn't disappoint! Right out of the gate, she scored twelve points, ten assists and had eight rebounds. The only downer of the night was that her team lost the game.

But afterwards, a special moment occurred. One of the parents in the stands walked over to Darcy and I and pointed to Marissa saying, "I can't believe your daughter is a freshman, she gets all of her teammates involved in the game like she's a senior out there. We got a real winner right there. Congratulations! Your daughter is going to be a great high school player!"

Soon after that exchange, a couple more parents approached us and said basically the same compliments. It made us feel comfortable about her being a student/athlete, and we felt confident she would have a wonderful high school experience.

Chapter XXII
Christmas and the Crash

We were now heading into the Christmas break, and at the time, I had two concerns. One concern was the Christmas bonuses for my employees. The other was learning about snowbirds.

The housecleaning business, as I learned, is sometimes seasonal. They have this term in the south, called snowbirds. I didn't understand it at first, as a matter of fact, it was real hard for me to figure out.

Growing up a northerner and becoming a southerner was a culture shock for us the first couple of years. With this job, I learned every year around October, I would get a couple of my clients calling me up and telling me, "Tony we're going on vacation, and we're going to miss a few cleanings, but we should return by April."

My response was, "Okay, where are you headed?" Most of them would say, Hawaii, Bahamas or an Alaskan cruise. I would say, "Thanks for letting me know, I'll make a note of it. I should expect you back in six months, correct?"

They would then say, "Yes, we do this every year around this time."

I would hang up thinking, they're going on a couple of cruises and they won't be back for six months. How am I to maintain my business income when I have clients leaving for such a long extended amount of time?

Then I would receive a call from another client around the same time. "Tony, this is Mrs. McCallister, I'm just calling to advise you that our service needs to be suspended for awhile. We should be back in March. We are going to see our kids in North Carolina."

"Thanks Mrs. McCallister. I'll see you back in March?"

She replied, "Yes, we always go away for the winter."

Now I'm thinking, Christmas is getting closer, and one call after another, I have clients leaving for a lengthy amount of time and my business income is slowly deteriorating. It was becoming a financial burden around the Christmas holidays, but I finally figured it out.

It's what healthy, wealthy, blessed, retired people do. Most of my clients were retired and had second homes all over the country. They would live in Florida for half of the year and somewhere else the other half. These were the snowbirds I was talking about.

The real problem every year however, was I couldn't figure out how many customers would leave year after year. This put a tremendous strain on business, my employees and my financial situation at home.

The first year I learned of this problem made Christmas time financially difficult and those Christmas bonuses I promised the employees became a worrisome. My intention was to give them all one hundred dollar bonuses. However, that amount had to be reduced because of the snowbird effect on my accounts receivable income. It was a real eye opening learning experience that I had to be concerned with every year during the holiday season.

After that experience, I learned to be more observant of the holidays and set some money aside during the year, for myself and those Christmas bonuses I promised. There's nothing more gratifying then being a business owner and seeing the joy on someone's face when you give that little extra to an employee during the holidays. I truly believe it has a huge effect on morale when your employees notice your compassion and contribution to their well being. To this day, Christmas bonuses remain an important part of our business success.

Upon entering two thousand seven, the future of our business was in question. The Stock Market crashed, along with our business. Another learning experience ensued.

Cleaning homes for some people is a luxury. I don't mean that in a condescending way, it's just reality. And, it's a fact.

Wealthy people wake up differently, live differently, think differently than your normal average not wealthy people. If they are retired, some play golf, every day. Some play cards, visit the pool regularly, play crochet, play tennis or basically stay home and do nothing. They're retired and wealthy. They have a better lifestyle than many regular average Joe senior citizens, God bless them, if it wasn't for them supporting me, I wouldn't have a business.

Please don't underscore what I am saying about them, they worked hard all their life to get into the position they are in and they deserve to live the lifestyle they dreamed of living. I understand that, and I am very grateful they have given me the opportunity to serve them. But, and a big but, most of them just don't want to clean their house. And, if they can afford to have someone do it for them, and their budget allows it, they will.

Then, there's the people who really do need someone to clean for them. For example, wealthy or not, people who are disabled, and the elderly. People who have two jobs and kids who can't afford much and can't maintain their home. People with allergies who can't tolerate cleaning products (when we clean their house, they leave for an extended amount of time until the odor disappears). The senior citizens who aren't financially secure because they depend on their social security check every month to make ends meet. The disabled who rely on their state disability check. All those scenarios of people are the ones I always felt compassionately obligated to help serve more. They are the backbone of all businesses.

The parents who work, the disabled who are sick and the elderly who are dependent, I would always try to give them the best possible price I could afford, without hurting myself. The one thing I always was aware of was not to be greedy. I always knew if you wanted to have a good business, compassion was a key component to implement into your business life.

You must realize one thing when you're in business. I don't care who it is or what they do, when it comes to food, mortgage/rent, family, car, those bills are everyone's top priority. Those needs are the first things that are going to get paid and prioritized in a financial crisis, guaranteed.

My situation was, I owned a cleaning business, and it was scary to think at the time, one of the last things in a financial crisis that won't matter to anyone, was money coming out of their budget for their house cleaning people. And in the middle of a bankruptcy plan, the last thing I needed and everyone else needed, was the two thousand seven stock market crash.

My thoughts were, if I could get out of this crisis, my business should survive the rest of my life. After that, I decided to work harder. I immediately put an ad in the local newspaper. It read, *"Don't let your house go dirty like the stock market, call Darcy's Cleaning Service, not only will you get a free estimate, but you will get your first housecleaning for free"*.

The idea was a gamble, but remember, I am a family owned business, and the beauty part about that was, I worked out of my garage. Which meant one thing, low overhead.

As other corporate cleaning companies were having a hard time paying their rent, I was paying nothing. I was able to reduce my costs and advertise at a lower price because the newspaper business was starving too. There were people who still wanted their house cleaned, but they couldn't afford to pay a lot of money and I knew that. If you remember, that was a time you saw a lot of double and triple coupons in the newspaper for grocery stores. There was a lot of buy one get one free dinners going on in the restaurants too. To me, this concept was the way to go. Yes, I was a small business, but I knew I had good instincts, and I was in survival mode.

Now, that's not to say, I didn't lose some good customers because I did. However, I gained some good ones too.

The one important key to know in small business or big business is to have the ability to adapt and change. I believe passionately, the most important thing is to have the patience and knowledge to accept a crisis situation when it's happening in your life. If you can apply that thinking you will be successful, if you decide to ignore the situation, it could have an explosive detrimental effect on your business to the point of no return.

The same thinking should be applied to your own life. If you cannot adapt to changes for the greater good, you will have a difficult time surviving. As I said before, in small business, greed is not good. Especially in a global financial crisis.

I became mentally prepared to beat my competitors at all costs. With kindness, respect and for a few dollars less. The results of that made us a little poorer for awhile, but we survived. Remember, we were in the middle of a bankruptcy crisis ourselves, our mission was to survive. We had a plan, because if you don't have a plan, you better pack your bags and get on your way. That's just the way it is. The world does not stop for you, and if you allow the world to control you, you will eventually succumb to ruins.

You have to fight adversity every day, and at the worst of times, you have to figure out a way to make life work. You have to dig deep into your heart, into your mind and into your soul. You need to pray every day that God helps you through a crisis. If you can do all that, you will surely increase your odds to survive so much better.

As everyone else was finding a way to make ends meet, I went the other way. I was trying to find a way to continue to build and grow my business. I came up with two big additions to add to my portfolio.

One, I was offering my base clients window cleaning treatments at a discounted price, while advertising in the newspaper for new customers at my regular price. It was a good way to make my clients feel they were getting a better deal than the outside customer.

The other idea was pressure washing. Everything from the entire exterior of a house to sidewalks, driveways, and screened in porches and lanais. You name it, I did it, anything to make money. I was able to manage these two new services because of the quality feedback I was getting from my housecleaning clients.

While the employees were servicing all their home cleaning needs, I was out in the field power washing their homes. In the end, my final sales totals went up twenty percent in a year of a financial banking crisis. I grew my business bigger and stronger by implementing those two extra services and the year turned out to be a pleasant surprise.

Chapter XXIII
The Process

Going into two thousand nine, I was understanding my business a little more now and how things worked. I would always try to look outside the box, and what I mean by that is, as a boss, I was trying to focus more on my employees and finding out what their needs were to be happy.

I would ask them, without bringing up money, how can I make things better for you? Most of them just wanted days off when they requested, and I would try my best to accommodate them. Surprisingly though, they would just ask for more hours.

The real surprise was when they would ask for better products to clean with. They would offer their opinion and say, better products make our work day easier. I appreciated and understood their input and took their suggestions to another level.

I started prioritizing new cleaning products that came out on the market. The ones that did a better job than the usual ones at a cheaper, not more expensive price. I learned the name on the bottle doesn't always mean it's the best product.

This was an important concern of mine because around this time, granite tops and stainless steel appliances were the new frenzy in the home market. Most people buying a new house back then wanted these upgraded extras. That became a very important detail because I had to acclimate myself to the market and supply my employees the new products the customers wanted. Again, that didn't mean I had to buy the most expensive products out there, just comparable ones at a better price.

My biggest concern with supplies were always vacuums. They were the most difficult to keep under budget, and the most used accessory. It was imperative that I found a good vacuum. One that was durable, long lasting and was made by a well known manufacturer at a reasonable price.

Of all the supplies we used, the vacuum was the most important concern to the clients and the most scrutinized. The most favored vacuums are the bagged vacuums, unfortunately manufacturers to this day, are still favoring the canister vacuums.

Then came Amazon. They were able to supply all my cleaning needs at a great cost. Thank you Amazon. With vacuums, they had the best choice, which was the Hoover Upright Tempo bagged vacuum. Now, by no means did that mean Hoover vacuums were the best, of course not. But they had the name, reputation and guarantee, plus they were reasonable. They worked great, and were easy to fix too.

I could buy a half dozen Hoover Upright Tempo vacuums for under four hundred dollars with Amazon, whereas the Tyson vacuums were four hundred dollars retail for one. That doesn't mean Tyson wasn't the better vacuum, it just meant I could get six Hoovers for the same price. After that, thanks to my employee's suggestions, I pretty much learned all the business scenarios I needed to know to grow the business even more.

As we were now entering our fifth full year, things were looking great for the future. Profitability was up every year since the stock market crashed, and I was hitting about twenty percent above my bottom line each subsequent year.

The next thing I implemented was raising prices. Something that people don't want to hear. I actually came up with a fantastic idea on how to make more money, give the employees raises, and put more money in the bank account without raising prices on my existing clients, and it worked great!

I started charging my second tier of new customers five dollars more for their service, while the original base of clients would stay at the same price. For example, if an original base client was paying sixty dollars for a three bedroom, two bath house, I would only propose a five dollar increase for the new perspective client, providing it was the same type of house, or close to it.

My thinking was, it was too risky to raise original clients that I was serving for such a short time. I didn't want to disrupt, threat or anger my original base because I couldn't afford to lose them. I knew if I wanted to continue growth in my business, I couldn't have a second tier of clients paying the same price. I had to keep establishing and growing accounts and sales, in order to keep up with salary demands, product supplies and expenses.

To offset these conditions, my idea was to offer something different to the new tier of clients in the new price negotiation process. In the beginning, when I was growing the business, I would handle an estimate as follows; negotiate the price, mark it down on my proposal sheet, see if they concurred by listening to their response, and see if they approved. Then I went on to say, "My estimate and my guarantee to you is I will never raise your price for services on your home once we agree. All you have to do is refer my service to a friend, relative or someone you know while servicing your home. If I get a new client from your recommendation, I will continue year after year, never to raise your price."

They would ask, "You can guarantee that?"

My answer would always be, "Yes."

Having that standard established, made my business have a steady growth, and strong foundation for the future. I had more flexibility, more to offer and the new sales pitch I was using was working consistently.

The idea behind this of course, was to continue to build the base, make a few more dollars and keep the older clients happy.

After that, I placed a new business rule into effect. If one year went by and I didn't get a new referral from them, I would then raise their cleaning price five dollars and only five dollars. This would grow the business and protect my foundation that I worked so hard establishing.

The second phase now was now complete. Next on the agenda, more importantly was to satisfy my employees. With the new base price being established, the price increases enabled me to give my first set of employees great raises, and I mean great raises.

Rule number one, if you want to keep good employees, I insist you make sure to give them what they deserve. Hard work, loyalty, and dependability don't come cheap. But the rewards are tremendous for your business.

Another thing I learned from Mr. Plangere was to pay your great employees their worth. Believe me, the good workers know what their worth is. Especially if they produce great results for you. Mr. Plangere use to say to me, if you implement that way of thinking, your business, your employees and your customers will be around forever.

Throughout my business career, year after year, I always would try to do what was best for my employees and my clients. I always knew that they were the foundation of my business, and if affordable, salary increases for my employees would really make the difference.

One lesson I learned for sure was; a pat on the employee back would only last so long, after awhile, that pat turns numb, and so does their dedication. No company, big or small, can avoid that one important issue. Money talks, or people walk, it's that simple and it always was my formula for success.

Chapter XXIV
Being Deaf, a Success

Business was going pretty good, and it felt like I was on auto pilot. Clients were happy, employees were happy. I had a good grip on how to keep this business rolling. My wife Darcy was doing great at All Souls Catholic School, her health was in great shape and she would always get home from work around four o'clock in the afternoon and I loved that.

After almost seven years now, the business was starting to run super smooth and I was finally able to quit Christian Care For Little Angels, the pre-school cleaning job I had in the afternoon.

But the best news at the time was from my kids. They were both having a banner year too. Michael, who was teaching eighth grade at Heritage Middle School in Deltona, decided to get married and buy a house, but that wasn't the best news.

One day he called and told me the Volusia County School District and the NASA Space program was interested in him, along with fourteen other teachers. They chose teachers from around the United States to fly into orbit on a space mission called "SOFIA".

The project was to move satellites that were out of position in the upper atmosphere, supplying radar technology to our solar energy farms on earth. I was ecstatic for him! Unfortunately, the great news only lasted a short while. A few months later the mission was deferred, realigned, and moved to another date for budget costs. However, after that, he was nominated for Teacher of the Year. We were so proud of his accomplishments.

Our daughter Marissa, was having a fantastic sophomore basketball season at Pine Ridge High School. In a game in early February, playing against Flagler High School, her play elevated to another level.

Not many people who are deaf, have the ability to take their talents to another level at any sport, much less basketball. But on this night in Flagler County, Florida, it was an accomplishment like none other. Darcy and I were so grateful we were there to witness it.

Most of that season, she was doing extraordinary things. Triple doubles were a common event for her, so were twenty point games, but that night, not only did she score a whopping thirty points, it was the way she was going about it.

Every time the opposing school, Flagler High School, scored a basket, she scored a basket. Every time Flagler came down to take the lead, she would find a way to get someone the basketball to score or score herself, and take the lead back. Every time she went to the free throw line, she was just automatic. Marissa was eleven for eleven at the free throw line that night. You don't need to know basketball to know what that means.

After the game that night, the opposing team players came up to her, congratulated her and were hugging her. Coach Palmer and her teammates were so proud of her because of her willingness to do whatever it took to win that ball game.

News about the game spread around the entire county the next day. The final tally box score for her that night was seven for nine from the floor, eleven free throws, nine assists, nine rebounds, thirty points. It was incredible!

The following game, two days later, another unbelievable game occurred. Something short of a miracle happened, and I'll never forget it.

Pine Ridge High School, Marissa's school, was playing against Mt. Dora High School in a meaningful district game in Mt. Dora, Florida. The gymnasium was standing room only that night. Everyone knew Pine Ridge was a good team and so was Mt. Dora. It was a battle of the two best 6A division teams in the county and a fierce rivalry.

The game ended up being a very physical, intense game. This game, would put my daughter on the map so to speak, as one of the best high school girls basketball players in the State of Florida.

In a very odd, strange and different way, Marissa was having another one of those great games. She had twenty-five points when the game went into overtime, and the place was rocking!

With a minute left to go in overtime, Coach Palmer wanted to slow the tempo down, and milk the clock down to ten seconds. The score was tied seventy-three to seventy-three when he called time out, with ten seconds left. He took the blackboard out on the sideline and chalked out a play to get the ball to Marissa. He wanted her to drive to the basket off a screen near the free throw line. Pine Ridge had the ball near their bench.

When the whistle blew, immediately the pass was thrown to her, she dribbled twice, got the screen from one of her teammates, then drove quickly to the basket. Immediately she was viciously fouled on the wrist and knocked to the floor with one second left on the game clock. The play worked perfectly! She was then awarded two free throws by the referee.

Then the Mt. Dora coach called time out. After the time out, the players came back onto the floor and what happened next was the most amazing thought by a human being I have ever witnessed on a basketball court. As I said, it was a packed house with a vocal, raucous crowd, almost deafening.

As Marissa stood at the free throw line, the referee tossed her the ball. She has two shots to win the game. At that moment, I look around realizing I was hearing words being screamed out so vile out of people's mouths in that basketball gym, like I never heard before. I never really felt bad for Riss when she was playing a game because Darcy and I made it a point to make her tough mentally and physically. We figured with a hearing disability, it was going to be tough on her already, so we tried to enforce confidence, strength, patience and faith throughout her entire life. But that night, I felt bad for her at that foul line. I wanted to get up and scream vile things myself to everyone there to defend her, but that just wasn't our style.

As she's standing there at the line with the ball, with people screaming at her, Mt. Dora players then start talking trash to her saying things like, you're gonna miss deaf girl!

She bounces the ball once, two bounces, then out of nowhere she stops. She looks over to me and Darcy, winks at us, looks at that crowd, and removes her hearing aids! She then shows the crowd her hearing aids, and puts them in her shorts pocket. Dear Lord, I was thinking, she can't hear. Then I said to myself, wait, I get this, she doesn't need to hear, the capacity crowd didn't know what to do. The deafening noise just got quiet.

First shot, Swisssh! Second shot, Swisssh! Game over. Pine Ridge wins, seventy-five to seventy-three!

The crowd went into a dead silence, except for the Pine Ridge families and players. We were all screaming for joy. I was saying to myself, my daughter who can't hear, just won the game! I then ran over to Marissa and gave her a big hug and said, "Nice move on the hearing aids." We both started to laugh.

The next day her picture was plastered all over the Daytona News Journal front page sports section, with a headline reading "NO SOUND EFFECTS".

Two nights later, another game, only this game was on television. That night she had another triple double, fourteen points, twelve rebounds, and ten assists.

After the game, the media came over to her and did a two and a half minute interview. Darcy and I were in the broadcast too. It's still a great You Tube moment!

The next day our phone was ringing off the wall with college coaches asking if she had committed to a university yet or if she had one in mind.

Then another incredible call. It was a coach from Wembley, England. He had seen Marissa's You Tube videos, and also viewed her on an exposure basketball web site, BeRecruited. He noticed she was one of the top basketball players in Florida. After a lengthy conversation, he offered Marissa an Overseas Pro Basketball contract paying twenty thousand dollars a year with all expenses paid. Only problem was, she had to give up all scholarship offers from colleges who were recruiting her.

After that call, we all sat down and agreed not to take the offer. Darcy and I always preached education first, so this decision was an easy decision for all of us.

At the end of the season, Marissa was awarded All Conference Team, All County Team and All State Team Honorable Mention. Not bad for a girl who is seventy percent hearing impaired.

That following summer it was all basketball. We figured, the more exposure playing in every tournament possible, the better the college offers. That's when team DEBO took over.

DEBO was an AAU State team that was made up of the finest high school AAU basketball players in the State of Florida and Marissa was slated into the starting point guard position.

The first tournament they entered was a warm up at Disney All Star Sports Complex. It was a successful tournament. Marissa played great and the girls took High Honors in two divisions.

Then came the Big South Classic. A big tournament held in North Carolina every year for the nation's top teams.

At this tournament, coaches from all around the country attend games at the University of North Carolina Chapel Hill, Duke University, and the University of North Carolina State. Their job is to recruit and focus on every player, while writing down notes and information on future players they would possibly make a scholarship offer to.

It was an astounding accomplishment by our daughter just to be there and be seen by all these college coaches. It was both rewarding and humbling at the same time. We knew if Marissa was at the top of her game, she would show well, but unfortunately, what was really apparent that day was her disability affecting her skill level. What I mean by that is, she was playing just as good as anyone out there, but there were distractions such as; playing in a game with other games being played side by side, because so many coaches needed to view so many players. The format was very difficult for her. Referee whistles blaring, extra balls bouncing, more vocalization everywhere, were really obstacles to overcome. The coaches noticed it too.

I remember one time when she was done with a game and walking off the court in a depressed state of mind we bumped into Coach Vivian Stringer of Rutgers. Coach Stringer was the second leading all time winning coach in the history of women's collegiate basketball. There she was, sitting under a basket. As we walked by her, she motioned to Marissa and said, "Sit down here, next to me honey." Then she asked, "You're deaf, aren't you?"

Marissa answered, "Yes Coach."

Coach Stringer than said to her, "You know, I've been playing, watching, and coaching this sport for over forty years, and I have never, ever seen a player like you before. Where did you get that determination from, probably your parents right?" While putting her arm around Marissa, she said, "Honey, I want you to remember one thing, and one thing only. The grace of God gave you a gift to play this sport with the best players out there in the country. No matter what happens, whether you get a scholarship or not, you have yourself to be proud of. Your disability gives people hope, they will notice that you have defeated all obstacles to get to this point in your life. You may not realize this now, but God may be using you as a tool for his own agenda. Take what comes, apply it to your life, like you have done with this game. I guarantee God will be there to reward you. Just follow your dreams."

I was completely and utterly in awe of this woman and what she said to my daughter. Needless to say, I'm a Vivian Stringer fan for life. How can I not be after the inspiring words she said to Marissa.

I went over and hugged Coach Stringer thanking her over and over again. I told her, "What an example of faith you have showed my family, God bless you Coach Stringer, it has been a pleasure, and a privilege to meet you."

Coach Stringer in a quiet voice then said to me, "She'll probably go Division Two, not Division One. These girls are far too big and tall for her."

I really appreciated that candor and honesty from her.

We left camp that day with such a wonderful feeling inside. We were so proud of our daughter, and it didn't even matter what college she chose to play at, just as long as she was happy where she ended up.

Chapter XXV
Managing and Growing a Small Family Business

After that basketball exposure and talking to Coach Stringer, managing my own life became even more important to me. I started to ask myself, when is your business big enough? My answer to that was, when you're not able to maintain personal attention to your relationship with your clients, employees, even with your friends and family. The roots of your business is important, but family should always be your top priority. Both started out small, and both were nurtured as they grew. It is important to understand, when things grow at a rapid pace, certain responsibilities tend to be forgotten.

In business, as well as a family, everyone wants to feel special. An employee wants to be recognized for their efforts and be compensated for it, justifiably so. A client wants to think they're the only client you have, and you better pay attention to them.

One thing I would never say to my client is, "Mrs. Smith, I really have to get going, I have another client waiting." It's like business suicide. Say that response to a client in any business and see how many customers you have left at the end of the year.

Then there's the most important thing, managing you and your family. Remember, you were the one to start your family and built it like your business. How irresponsible would it be for you not to give it the attention it deserves? You can call that family suicide.

Your business relies on you to get that important job. It was you who built the foundation. Your family relies on you to support them. Not paying any attention to either one of them will eventually have negative results.

This past year in my life, I reflected, evaluated and took a back seat. I realized I was getting very busy and other responsibilities needed to be more prioritized.

With my daughter, college was on the horizon and where she was going to play basketball. With my son Michael, after buying his first house he sometimes needed my advice and help. And as for the Catholic Church Darcy and I attend, they were now asking me to become more involved.

My thoughts on that were, when church asks of you, God is calling you to help. There were several requests for missionary help, but the most important to me, was being an Extraordinary Minister of Holy Communion of the Catholic Church (EMHC). God was calling on me to serve his people the Body and Blood of Jesus Christ, and there was no way I was going to deny that.

I took everything into consideration, my responsibilities as a husband, a father, and business owner and made a decision. I had to find a balance to make it all work. I started to minimize my work labor part of life so I could free up some time for my own personal life.

Up until this point, I have been running the business for about eight years and it was time to start handing over more of the work load to my employees. However, I couldn't dismiss the ole saying, *If you want something done right, then do it yourself.* That saying does hold a lot of truth. My clients would always make me think of that line when they would say to me, "I don't know what it is Tony, but when you get done cleaning my house, I see a difference in your work compared to any of your employees who have cleaned my home."

In a way, it's a very nice compliment to hear, but in reality, what it really means is, if you don't find a way to reinforce your clients confidence in your employees, it could become very critical in continuing to build your business. At some point you need to make the client feel you have confidence with your employees and they're wrong for thinking that.

Whenever I would hear that line being said, I would immediately bounce it back by saying, "Oh no, Mrs. Smith, excuse me for saying this, but I was the one who trained them, and it is because of them my business has grown. My employees are very capable people and I owe them much gratitude for being not only the people they are, but the workers that I appreciate so much."

By saying that, I took the emphasis off of me, and in a positive way showed my clients the confidence I had in my employees. I knew I had to establish this because I had to reduce my workload and take on other projects in my life. My clients needed to hear that I had complete trust, and faith in my business concept. At that point, I then started to reduce my workload and started to focus more and more on personal attention to everyone in my life.

Chapter XXVI
Don't Ever Get to Comfortable

We all fall into this trap. Just when you think life is going smoothly, something always comes around to test your will, confidence and faith.

For me two thousand ten was another one of those years. I was getting comfortable, I mean, why not? Business was going great, Darcy was healthy, not a cancer scare in sight. Marissa was deciding which university to choose. Her choices were down to Texas or Virginia. My son Michael and his wife were on the verge of starting their own family.

On a beautiful Florida night, Darcy and I were out on the lanai having a cup of coffee, when I suddenly get a telephone call from New Jersey.

It was my dad's friend, Tanya. She calmly explained to me that my dad's health was a concern and he was having a hard time breathing. One of his doctors suggested that he relocate down to my house in Florida so I could take care of him.

For me, this was a no brainer, but as I have said before, balance is a key thing in your life. I told Tanya, "Let me talk to Darcy about this and I will get back to you. I just need to figure a few things out."

If this news about my dad's health wasn't bad enough, the phone rings the next day and its Coach Palmer calling me from practice. Frantically, he yelled at me saying, "Tony, you better get your butt to the gym fast, Marissa hurt her knee to the point where we had to call an ambulance."

With a dreadful feeling in the pit of my stomach, I responded, "Okay Coach, please have the ambulance wait for me, I will be there in ten minutes!"

When I arrived at the gym I saw Riss lying on the court crying. Not complaining so much about being in pain, she was mostly worrying about the scholarship offers she received last week to play in Virginia and Texas.

I told her not to worry, it will be alright, everyone hurts their knee at some point in this game, you're no different. Let's get to the hospital and see what they say.

Now, that's what I told her, but I feared the worst. I was thinking it was an ACL (Anterior Crucial Ligament) injury, which I knew would be devastating.

I got into the ambulance with her, called Darcy and Michael to tell them what was happening. I was trying to keep Marissa as calm as possible and within fifteen minutes we arrived at the hospital.

She was taken immediately in for x-rays. About a half hour later the bad news was revealed. A complete knee reversal of the meniscus and patella (knee cap), with torn ligaments and cartilage damage. However, the main injury we were concerned about, the ACL, was unharmed. So there was some hope. I knew though, there was going to be extensive rehab therapy set into place.

The other problem for her was the college coaches in Virginia and Texas who offered her scholarships. They had to be notified about the injury because of the possible affect it would have on her basketball abilities. The plan was to get her healthy as soon as possible.

She needed to get the knee strength and muscles back to normal. Then after that her skill levels needed to be reevaluated. It was imperative to quickly get her rehab schedule set into place because April is the month where most high school athletes sign their intent to play sports in college.

In Marissa's case, we already knew the schools that were interested in her, Austin College in Texas and Hollins University in Virginia. Unfortunately, as the process was being determined where she was going to play, some of the other schools that were interested in her dropped out for the same two reasons. One was when they heard about her knee injury, the other reason was because of her hearing impairment. But that wasn't going to deter her, if anything it made her stronger in mind and heart to get back on the court sooner than later. My job was to make sure she didn't rush into playing and reinjuring that knee.

Upon signing day, the two universities unfortunately weren't ready to sign her yet. They wanted to see a glimpse of how that knee was repairing and what effect it had on her game.

Then one day in May of two thousand ten, the coach from Hollins University in Virginia called up and asked Marissa, "How are you feeling?"

Riss replied, "I feel great Coach, ready to run a game now."

Coach Waggoner then told her, "I'm glad you said that. We want to make sure you're physically and mentally prepared to play before you sign that scholarship offer. Do you think your parents can get you here this weekend for a run through practice?"

She excitedly told him, "No problem Coach, they would be happy to do that."

When she got off the phone with him, she explained to us what he wanted. We said of course we will drive you there this weekend.

I knew this was a tryout. I also figured what she did at practice that day would determine if they were going to sign her or not.

That Wednesday we get a telephone call from the Athletic Department. The Athletic Director said, "We have a guest room for parents on campus. Would you like to leave early and enjoy the weekend on us?"

Pleasantly surprised we replied, "That was very thoughtful of you." We thanked him for his offer and accepted.

We arrived there on Thursday afternoon, took a tour around campus and made sure Marissa was well rested.

The next morning we brought Riss down to the gym for the team practice and to meet with the coaches. The coaches immediately approach us and said, "Good morning Mr. and Mrs. Cimino, so nice to meet you. We will take Marissa from here. Go out and have some breakfast, come back in a couple of hours and then we'll talk."

At breakfast, Darcy and I both agreed that today's practice will determine whether our daughter goes to school here or not. We were right because after practice was finished, Coach Waggoner immediately met us outside the gym without Marissa.

First thing he said was, "I want to tell you both what a remarkable job you did bringing up your daughter. It's one thing to raise a daughter who is a basketball player, but with a hearing impairment, I can't imagine. She played unbelievable today! Just to let you know, we played a simulated game not a practice."

Immediately I told him, "At breakfast we talked and figured that's what you were going to do today and we understood that."

Coach Waggoner continued, "Our idea was to put her on the second team and have her play against the first team. Our mindset was, if she can perform at a high level today, then our questions would be answered. Bottom line was, she went out and scored twenty-seven points, five assists, one turnover. She was amazing!" While grinning ear to ear, Coach Waggoner then said, "We would love to have her come to our school next year."

Needless to say, Darcy and I were ecstatic! We then told him, "We would be honored to have our daughter play for you coach."

"Great. I'll let her know what you both said, and then I will meet you all at the Administration building in ten minutes. They have something there you might want to fill out."

When we get to the Administration building, the Athletic Director, financial aid assistant, along with Head Coach Waggoner, escort Darcy and I into the Athletic Director's office. Coach Waggoner, in a humoristic way, said, "Before we start this meeting, I think it would be a good idea to wait for Marissa."

No sooner than he said that, Marissa walked in the door. Immediately, Coach Waggoner looked at Marissa and said, "Young lady, what a joy it would be for us to have you play next year for Hollins University."

Coach Waggoner then looked over at Darcy and I and asks, "Mr. and Mrs. Cimino, everyone feels this school would be the perfect fit for your daughter, therefore, I'll get right to it. Hollins University would like to offer Marissa a seventy-five thousand dollar Presidential scholarship. If, of course, Marissa accepts."

Needless to say, we were stunned and overwhelmed. As parents, we prayed about this moment many times during our life and I was thinking the whole time we were here, God has a plan for her, I just didn't know where it was heading.

Here she was five months ago laying on the ground not knowing if she would ever play again, and now she's signing to play collegiate basketball along with having an unbelievable opportunity to have her education paid for in the process. We were so proud of her. How could we not be thanking God?

Like any other parents, we walked out of the office screaming and hugging each other, and then we visited the campus clothing store to buy practically every Hollins University shirt money could buy.

About a month later, we received more good news. My dad's condition improved. What a blessing that was! His doctors were optimistic about his health and felt he would be fine staying in New Jersey.

It was certainly a roller coaster ride for the first six months of the year.

Now that we knew where Marissa was attending college, it was time to implement a new business model and work on my third tier of potential clients.

The philosophy again was, don't raise prices on the second tier base clients, but raise prices five dollars on new perspective clients. The plan remained the same, my sales pitch again was, "If you accept my proposal, I will never raise your price as long as you recommend my service."

My business currently had about fifty homes we serviced on a weekly and bi-weekly basis. Next on the agenda was to focus on building a portfolio of monthly clients. I restructured the cost factors and adjusted them accordingly, to have monthly clients pay a premium price. The higher premium price would be charged because more work and time was needed to clean their home.

The monthly cleans were always difficult to estimate on a cost basis. There were so many variables that had to be considered. How dirty does this house get every month? How long will it take to clean it? Is this new potential client maintaining their house on a consistent basis?

Taking all of this into consideration, I came up with a fifty percent formula. For example, a regular client who has their house cleaned on a bi-weekly schedule is paying seventy-five dollars. For a monthly clean on the same size house, I would charge the monthly client forty dollars more, for a total cost of one hundred fifteen dollars a clean.

Of course, in the beginning, it was a trial and error basis, but it seemed like the proper cost to charge for a house that was scheduled to be serviced only once a month.

Another problem I inherited about accepting monthly clients was there always was a threat they would cancel the service right after the first clean. Two reasons came into play. One, they would find another competitor at a cheaper price or during the estimate, they would lead me to believe they wanted a routine monthly clean. In reality, some only wanted their house cleaned for a party or an event and they only wanted to pay the monthly rate.

I quickly caught onto this and I learned to adjust the problem when conducting an estimate.

Two, while performing a proposal for a perspective monthly client, I would now ask questions such as, are you having a party soon or is this a one-time clean? Did you have family visiting recently and just want us to come over once and clean your home, or would you like your house to be cleaned on a regular monthly basis?

During these conversations, I really had to pay attention to the customers direction because to this day, I occasionally get mislead and can't determine their desires. I also have to be more observant of the conditions of their homes.

Important business model 101, during an estimate, always listen to people who want your business. Pay close attention to their wants, needs and schedule. During an estimate, listening to a perspective client could be very crucial in determining the success of your business.

I learned to be more open and up front with the potential clients during the negotiation process. I would basically interview them and honestly discuss the overhead. I would explain my costs and what I could afford to negotiate. I would then explain to them half the amount you pay goes to salary and expenses. Taxes, products, supplies, gas, and insurance are all part of my costs. I would make them realize and understand they're not just paying a person to clean their home, they're paying for a service to fulfill their cleaning needs.

I would then compose an estimate for the cleaning of their home. If they were not satisfied with my estimate, I would think outside the box, just to get their business. I would offer them something different to consider. It could be a two hour, two employee time limit, or a four hour, one employee time limit. That would help to keep their cost down.

I would intently try and make them aware that I understood their budget and their situation. However, I also made them aware of my side of the business and the details of how I propose an estimate.

Most of the time this technique worked. Sometimes it did not, but most of all they appreciated my openness and honesty in the negotiation process.

When I was finished, they would at least assure me a good recommendation because of the time and patience I spent with them explaining my business procedures.

Moving into the following year, I implemented more new cost factors. The most important thing I learned during that time was to be reasonable, patient and understanding and not fluctuate prices.

I was surprised to learn how many clients talked to one another about my pricing. The term word of mouth came into play numerous times among my clients. The positive feedback and recommendations from my clients, were by far the stronghold for growing my company.

Chapter XXVII
Offer More, Accept Setbacks

How do you continue to grow your business without raising prices too high or estimating to low? Thinking back in the beginning when I first started the business, I would charge initial cleaning fees on first time cleans. This was a one-time charge higher than the actual weekly or bi-weekly cleaning fee.

When I would walk into a house that has not been cleaned in years and seeing the condition of it, I would have to make price adjustments. I needed to charge more than the regular standard set price because the homes needed more extensive, detailed work. For example; wiping down wood molding, door handles, finger prints on doors, wiping down vertical blinds or plantation shutters. Some clients may want their patio swept, their furniture vacuumed, beds made, sheets changed, and interior windows washed.

Realizing time is costly on all of these details, instead of charging initial cleaning fees, I came up with the idea to have an extra item charge. I would apply a ten dollar service fee for any extra item they wanted above and beyond their normal cleaning.

As years passed, and the business was established, I removed the charge and would offer some of these extra items for free, as a courtesy for being a loyal client. My only request was that they would let me know in advance which extra they wanted so I could schedule my employees accordingly.

I would present this to my perspective clients during the estimation process. It was my "buy-in" advertisement I offered them. This gesture made the new client understand I really wanted their business.

However, with this offer, I also learned a valuable lesson. There were drawbacks to that kind of negotiation. Some people would often take advantage of my kindness and generosity, which forced me to start drawing lines on what I could offer a new perspective client. My thinking and process needed to be changed.

From then on, I had to decide which extra item was going to be applied as a courtesy, or applied for a service fee. Negotiating these buy-ins eventually became a determent. It was my own fault and it was time to correct the damage that was done.

Some perspective clients actually thought I was taking advantage of them. They felt I was being aggressive and trying to persuade them to use my company just to make a sale.

Another problem I had to correct was when I had two employees service a home and it would take more than three hours to clean. I would ask my employees why it took that length of time with two people cleaning. They would advise me that the client had asked for certain extras to be done and that I approved it.

My workers would go on and tell me, "You always made it a point to us, if a client requests an extra item to be done, just satisfy them and do it. Because of that, it took us an extra hour to clean today."

That was something I always told my employees. Customer satisfaction was very important to me. However, because of scenarios like that, it was time for me to explain to the customer exactly what the housecleaner was responsible for, while paying for a standard cleaning service.

This problem had to be addressed immediately. I learned clients were never concerned about cost factors on my end, their only concern was getting their house cleaned the way they wanted it. I had to know the cost factors involved, that was my job.

While estimating a two story home, I knew it would take two hours for each employee on the average to clean. To figure out the cost factor, I first had to know the salary payout. Paying each employee twelve dollars an hour (which is around the approximate salary for a house cleaner), the job would cost forty-eight dollars in salary payout. Then you need to figure in travel, insurance, taxes and product costs.

The margin for profit in this business should be anywhere from forty-three to forty-eight percent. That means just with salary payout for this house, you would have to charge more than ninety dollars to hit those margins. That estimate doesn't make for a very good profit, does it?

The only way you can avoid a loss in this situation is to have one employee clean that home. However, you're opening yourself up to other issues such as; will the employee be finished in a timely fashion so they can get to their next job.

For all this to work out and have a margin of forty-three percent, a twelve dollar an hour employee would have to clean that two story house in three and a half hours.

That is why it is so important to be very diligent, accurate and professional with your estimates. Remember, you are the owner and you set the rules. If there is an issue with pricing, you need to put the blame on yourself.

Chapter XXVIII
Cycles

Over the years as the business was growing, I was continually learning the bargaining and negotiating process. Be that as it may, life was getting ready to throw another curve ball at us. Another one of those dreadful cycles was coming. Another test was presented that we would have to endure and hopefully pass.

I learned, painfully, this life we live is all about cycles. Some are good, some bad, some long, some are short. Whatever the case, they come and come again, without a moment's notice. Which brings me to Thanksgiving, two thousand ten. A Thanksgiving my family would want to forget.

Over the long holiday weekend we were attending our daughter Marissa's basketball game at Hollins University. There were about three games she was playing in a four day span.

Prior to our visit, we called the University and asked them if we could reserve a room in the parent house on campus. The room was reserved for us and we left for Virginia.

We arrived in time to have dinner with Marissa and a few of her basketball teammates. It seemed like it was going to be a pleasant, exciting weekend. The weather was beautiful and Darcy and I had some quality time off. We were really looking forward to relaxing and watching Marissa play.

After dinner and discussing basketball for about an hour, the girls went back to their dorm to get ready for the game. We were so content and happy just to be there. We walked over to the campus coffee shop to get a cup of coffee and got to the gym around seven o'clock, fifteen minutes before the game started. We were taking the experience all in, being proud parents, our daughter playing a game she loves and remembering all the time, work and effort we all put in getting her here. That happy, content feeling was all about to change.

On the opening tip, after the jump ball occurred, the ball flew over to the free throw line and was loose on the ground. While rolling down the court it looked like it was going to roll out of bounds.

Several players were chasing after the ball for possession and we notice one of the players was Marissa. The other two players were from Roanoke University.

As the ball was quickly heading out of bounds, we saw all three girls leap and dive for the ball.

At that moment, a horrifying scream is heard. The gym suddenly gets quiet and the players are motioning to the coaches to come over. I could hear my heart pounding in my chest and the moment seemed frozen in time.

I couldn't believe what I was seeing again. Our daughter lying on the ground grabbing her knee. The same knee she had injured before.

The coach then calls and motions me over and says, "Mr. Cimino, the athletic trainer seems to think it's a separation of the same meniscus that was rehabilitated in February. We're going to get her up, wrap her in ice and get her evaluated. I'll see you at half time."

I was stunned. I didn't even know how to react to the situation. It was one of those moments you don't even have time to think. But just listening to the trainers quick diagnosis made me feel this injury may never heal back to normal again.

After talking to the coach at half time he said, "It looks pretty serious. You might want to call your doctor tomorrow. You may want to bring her back home to see an orthopedic surgeon for a better diagnosis. I think she's done with basketball for awhile."

After hearing this news we didn't think matters could get any worse, but that wasn't the case.

The next day, which also happened to be our thirtieth wedding anniversary, was not a day to celebrate. While getting ready to head home, we received a telephone call from Marissa's guidance counselor. She asked if we could come down to the Administrative building that morning.

When we arrived, the secretary brought us into an office. Already in there were some administrative staff, Marissa's coach, her trainer, and the Athletic Director.

Looking around confused I said, "Excuse me, if you don't mind me asking, what is this meeting all about?"

First, they all introduced themselves and were very pleasant and cordial to us. However I could tell we were there for something else other than Marissa's injury. It was a quiet, somber room and we felt more bad news was on the way.

Marissa's guidance counselor spoke first and said how proud they were of Marissa's accomplishments and what a joy it was to have her here playing on campus. Then the boom hit. She continued, "However, her studies and grades have faltered below our expectations and we can no longer support her scholarship and education here at Hollins University."

Needless to say, we were very upset and dumbfounded to hear this news. I asked them, "What about the tutoring and the note taking Marissa was supposed to receive?"

They immediately responded telling us they have exhausted all means of special aid and felt her hearing impairment was dramatically affecting her ability to keep up with the regimen they required. They couldn't apologize enough for their decision.

The guidance counselor went on to say, "Being a student athlete has demands and when there is a scholarship involved it was their responsibility to protect the integrity of their school. Your daughter is no different, disability or not. Every student/athlete on this campus has the same demands, therefore when making a decision like this, it is not only to protect our sports program but it also is out of concern for our student's education."

Hearing this decision was hard to accept. We felt the school made this decision based on the combination of the injury sustained, the inability to perform well in her studies, along with her hearing impairment.

I couldn't explain how awful I felt for my daughter. She was so upset. She worked so hard practicing, five hundred shots a day in the driveway, almost every day of her life. Studying, putting the extra time into her school work. It all came crashing to an end that day.

Everyone tried to console her by saying how proud they were of her, and what an accomplishment it was with her disability to even get to this level, but to no avail. At the time, Marissa really didn't want to hear them.

Darcy and I tried to make her understand, this was not the end of the road. Instead, it was a time to reflect, move on and be thankful for what you achieved. It was a time to learn there will be adversities in your life and you must learn how to cope with them when they come along.

We told Marissa the most important thing right now was to get back home and get that knee healed. We also let her know not to give up on school, she could enter Community College which would be more apt to implement a program for her hearing disability.

The following day, we left for home and immediately made an appointment with her orthopedic doctor.

This entire experience was devastating for Marissa. One day your at the university of your choice, playing basketball, a game you love, while dreaming of maybe someday playing professional basketball, and the next day, you wake up, and you're going home for good!

Trying to console Marissa, I told her, "You never know in life, there are no guarantees, but that's the way life is. Everyone has adversities, but in the end you must realize that this time too shall pass, and as always, by placing your trust in God, He will find a way to move you into a positive direction."

I felt it was important to explain to her there is life without basketball, and with her vivacious personality, wonderful opportunities would lie ahead for her.

Marissa did not have to undergo surgery, however, she had six months of strenuous, rigorous rehabilitation. I knew it was going to be tough on her, and it was tough. She was first diagnosed in rehab as only having forty percent movement in her knee. But through demanding sessions of treatment, the rehabilitation therapy was a success.

As expected, Marissa's knee healed, and she was back to normal. We told her how proud we were of her and how well she handled her therapy. Again, our advice to her was, God has a plan for you.

At that time, we didn't know where God was taking her, but we always had this feeling her disability would lead her to helping others or just to help someone who is in need of a warm heart. Our thoughts were confirmed, however, she took a very unusual path.

When her rehabilitation was complete, her stubbornness, willingness and desire to play basketball again got the best of her. Like any other athlete, she had a difficult time giving up a sport she loved so much. She intended to give basketball another try.

One afternoon, when I got home from work, Marissa ran to greet me and excitedly said, "Dad, I contacted Coach Gina from DEBO and I persuaded her to give me another opportunity to practice with them! Maybe I can play competitive basketball again!"

"Coach Gina approved that?"

"Yes," said Marissa.

"I'm surprised. She knows the extent of your injury."

Then Riss explained, "She hesitantly agreed Dad. But she knows how much basketball means to me."

"Okay, but only because it's Coach Gina."

It was finally the day of practice. When we arrived at the gym, Coach Gina immediately came over to us.

Coach Gina, is a very impressive coach, who stands six feet two inches tall, with long blonde hair and a muscular physique that could rival Arnold Schwarzenegger.

Coach Gina immediately voiced her opinion to me and said, "Mr. Cimino, Marissa called me. I'm not in favor of this idea, however, I know how much she loves this game. I am willing to give her a try, but trust me, if I see or feel she is not physically capable of keeping up with this practice, I will quickly put a stop to it."

I knew in my heart this is what Marissa wanted, and listening to Coach Gina made me feel confident she had Marissa's best interest in mind. Besides, do you think I'm going to question a six foot two blonde Arnold Schwarzenegger, I don't think so.

So I gave her my approval. Immediately after our conversation, she went over to Marissa on the court and said to her, "Riss, at anytime we feel your knee is not capable to withstand simple moves during play, I will immediately stop practice and let you know it's too dangerous for you to continue."

After about fifteen minutes of DEBO's demanding practice, it was apparent that Marissa's knee wasn't responding the way it should for basketball.

One test that indicated this was the explosion test. This required the player to dribble the ball quickly past another player in just a few tenths of a second. Her quickness was gone.

Another simple drill Coach Gina tested her on was one-on-one play, not allowing an opponent to score. That was unsuccessful. After a few other simple techniques, Marissa was able to figure it out on her own. Basketball was definitely out of the question.

I could see the look in Coach Gina's eyes, it was hard for her not to tear up. Marissa was one of her favorite ballplayers.

Coach Gina gave Marissa a huge hug. We then thanked Gina and all the players for giving her an opportunity to try to play. We told them how much we appreciated everything they did to contribute towards her basketball career.

It didn't take long for Marissa to focus on a new career path. At dinner one night, she said to Darcy and I, "I've been doing a lot of thinking lately and just in case my practice with DEBO didn't work out......"

I interrupted her and said, "What's in your head Riss?"

Marissa hesitantly went on to ask, "Is it okay to take a break from college for awhile? I want to figure out what to do next with my life. There's never been a moment in my life without basketball. I wanted to try something different, so I recently put in an application with Carnival Cruise lines, and I got an email back from them today. And you're never going to believe this, but they want me to work as an entertainer on their ship! The ship they want me on docks at the Port of Miami and sails to the Caribbean. I'm really excited about this opportunity! How do you both feel about that?"

Stunned, my response was, "A cruise ship, out on the sea, you got to be kidding!"

Not Darcy though, she was excited for her, and laughing about it. Needless to say, I found myself outnumbered.

For the next year and a half, Marissa worked at Carnival Cruise Lines. After working out of the Port of Miami, she was transferred to the Port of Los Angeles, California, sailing to Hawaii and Alaska and the Mexican Riveria.

Her job was to entertain the passengers by hosting shipboard events such as; Karaoke, Bingo games, trivia games, and even singing and dancing in Broadway type shows. The work was hard, but she was having a blast, eventually earning two thousand dollars a month with all expenses paid.

Yes, my hearing impaired daughter was working on a cruise ship. Did I not say earlier that God had a plan for her? I eventually warmed up to the idea. We even sailed with her on her ship a few times for a discounted fare. Go figure.

Yes, life was going pretty well for my daughter and I was very happy for her to, say the least.

Life is full of cycles and unfortunately another sad cycle was approaching.

While Marissa was off working on her Carnival Cruise ship, we received some upsetting news.

My dad's friend Tonya called and said, "Tony, your dad had a major heart attack and you need to get back to Jersey immediately."

I didn't know what was going on at the time, last report I had, he was doing pretty well. However, hearing the distress in Tonya's voice didn't give me a good feeling.

I felt like the phone call came a little too late for me to get back there in time to see him.

I immediately took the first available flight out of Orlando, Florida. It seemed like the longest flight ever. All I kept thinking about was my life with my dad, and knowing when I get there, it might be the last time I see him.

When I landed, I was able to get my rental car quickly and headed straight to the hospital. When I arrived at the hospital, admissions told me he was on the fourth floor cardiac care unit. That wasn't good news to hear.

As the elevator on the fourth floor opened, Tonya was there waiting for me. She grabbed my arm, and was rushing me to his room.

As I entered his room, I saw Father Gerard standing at his bedside. Right away, I knew that was not a good sign. Then I noticed my dad had tubes everywhere on his body. It was extremely difficult for me seeing my dad in that condition.

I could vividly remember when I was young, this strong Italian man who once had biceps the size of tree trunks, and hands like a vice when you shook them. Just the mere thought of his left eye going up made you think you were in some kind of trouble.

Now there was nothing I could say or do to help him. It was out of my hands and placed into God's hands.

With tears streaming down my cheeks, I softly grabbed his hand, and thanked him for everything he taught me, said to me, and how much he influenced my life. I kissed his forehead and said, I love you dad.

Then Father Gerard took his other hand and we prayed the Our Father together. I heard my Dad take one long, last breath, and then he was gone.

My dad was eighty-seven years old. His death was a blow in my life, but it didn't seem too devastating for some reason. It was kind of a numbing feeling and sad for lots of different reasons.

I was thinking how my whole life, my dad was a tough Italian family man, brought up in a generation of war and poverty, where three jobs were necessary to raise a family. Back then, hugs and kisses were not a man's make up. If you were a son, you were going to work, if you were a daughter, you were marrying a guy who will work. That's the way it was for an Italian family, plain and simple.

My feelings were my Dad lived a good life, eighty-seven years old. I've seen so many family members die so young and so painfully, somehow his death was easier for me to cope with, in some sort of strange way. Maybe it was because of being raised in a manly type of way, that's the way he wanted me to feel.

Then I started thinking of my mom dying at fifty-four years old, pretty close to the same age as my brother. My Grand-mom was sixty-seven and Grand-pop was fifty-two. I started thinking about Darcy's mom. She was sixty years old when she past. Her two sisters who were twenty-five and thirty-seven years old, all battling and succumbing to cancer.

It really did humble both Darcy and I and made us realize how blessed and fortunate we were as a couple to still be alive. So I guess when my dad passed away, I felt grateful for having him around as long as I did.

The most important thing I was focused on at this time, was to make sure I had a Catholic funeral mass for my dad. That was one of the promises I made to him. Another promise I made was for him to be buried next to my mom. I also promised him I would always try to keep the family together.

The final promise I had to make to my dad was to make sure before I die, to take Darcy to Rome, Italy. There were many reasons for this last request, but the most important reason was, he wanted his only son left to see where all the family roots began and he wanted Darcy and I to visit the place that was special to him and to us, St. Peter's Basilica, at the Vatican. But I took it one step further.

Chapter XXIX
The Man, the Million, the Miracle

After my father's passing, I tried to be optimistic as always, and made sure life continued in a positive direction. In the year two thousand fourteen, so many good things happened to us. It was time to celebrate!

First, Marissa was finishing out her last contract on the cruise ship, and was coming home for good. Then my son's wife, Caryn, delivered our second grandchild. Darcy's doctor gave her a clean bill of health and was given an excellent diagnosis for her future. And as for myself, a man who at one time flipped pizzas, cut lawns, repossessed cars, cleaned post offices, sold shoes, worked for a newspaper, and was told he couldn't get a job, somehow, miraculously managed to surpass the one million dollar sales mark with a mop, a bucket and a housecleaning service with a woman's name at the top of the business card!

By no means am I claiming I'm a millionaire, however, who could of ever dreamed that a man, with a mop, who cleans homes, could earn a million dollars in sales!

If anyone ever said to me twenty years ago, quit your newspaper job and pick up a mop, you're going to earn a million dollars, I would have thought they were nuts!

But it's been fourteen years now, and it really has happened. I never ever thought with all the hardships we endured, this could happen, but it has. God has blessed us abundantly!

I often think if my mom was around, what would she say. But believe it or not, before she died, she actually was cleaning houses to make extra money. That is what's so ironic.

As for my dad and my brother, well, if my brother knew, it wouldn't have surprised him, he always knew I

261

was a hard worker. And if my dad knew, he probably would of said, well your grandfather sold fruits and vegetables on a Brooklyn street corner, so I guess you did what you had to do to survive. I could hear my Dad saying that to me all the time as I cleaned people's homes.

I am very grateful for those people in those homes too. They have supported my family over the years and have been very loyal clients, some staying with our service since the beginning. That's the one thing about having personal relationships, especially in business. There has to be a trust factor there all the time, and your reputation is so important. The stronger the trust and reputation, the better the business.

In the years I have been working as a small business owner, what really surprised me the most was the word of mouth only recommendation. It is a very strong advantage to have.

Many businesses are corporate driven and depend on volume and advertisement, sort of like Amway or Mary Kay. They hire an abundance of sales people to sell their products, then they hire more sales people who earn a commission selling their products, then they hire even more sales people to keep up the pace and volume of sales. Always concerned about hitting that next projected dollar amount their supervisors demand. That takes time, effort, progress and money to get the word out.

With a small family business, it's just you and your reputation to build on. You need to hire great employees, establish a friendly atmosphere, throw some trust in there and do a couple of favors for them now and then. That's what makes a small business a successful business. As I said before, greed destroys businesses and relationships.

In the beginning, you must take it slow, sacrifice, and by all means show a love for your business. This will have a positive effect on the employees you hire and your clients who hire you. This formula has consistently worked for me, and I hope by sharing it with you, it works for you too.

The most important thing by far though, is faith and trust in God. Through good times and bad, you must be resilient, steadfast and confident. God will show you the way.

As you have now read, all my life, I have put my faith in God, and all my trust into Him. And when those horrific cycles came, He was the one I would pray to immediately for help.

In two thousand fifteen my wife and I celebrated something I never, ever thought would of been possible twenty years ago. On November twenty-second two thousand fifteen, we were married thirty-five years.

Two kids, growing up in a small town in Neptune, New Jersey, who didn't go to college, but always had a dream to start their own family someday. We managed to stay faithful and happily married. For us, it was never about the money, but it always has been about our love, respect and trust for one another. Our goal on our anniversary that year, was to renew our vows to show God how important he really was in our lives.

Chapter XXX
Our Dreams Come True

Those long talks I mentioned before about my dad before he died, were spoken for a reason. It was years of growing up in an Italian household with an Italian father who came from Naples, Italy, where our Catholic faith was so important.

Back in the day in Italy, you went to church on Sunday, no excuses. As my dad was growing up, my grandfather passed that importance onto my dad and he made sure he passed it onto me. No matter how poor they were back then, or how much they worked to survive, and what little they had in food and clothing, no matter what, you were always going to thank God for everything at church on Sunday.

When my Grand-pop and Grand-mom came to America to work and raise a family, this was one important staple they were going to attach to our lives forever.

As for Darcy's family, God was important in their lives too, and she was raised in the same Catholic faith. I truly believe that is what ultimately attracted us.

We were both popular kids in high school, we both played sports (Darcy had a love for hockey). We both worked jobs while growing up, and we both earned everything ourselves, without asking for anything from our parents. We really had a lot in common. Our goal was to raise a family and live according to the Bible and what God asked from us. Our parents knew this, and they were both in favor of our marriage.

Were there awful circumstances surrounding our wedding, absolutely. But where was our wedding at? In a church, on the altar, in front of God, with family present.

On our thirty-fifth wedding anniversary, I made that last promise to my father a reality and I took Darcy to Rome, Italy.

Going to Italy was a life-long dream, as it was for most of our family. They too had their dream to visit Rome someday in their lifetime, to see where the foundation of where our family began. However, as time went by, physically and financially it became more difficult for them and one by one as they passed, so did their dreams.

As I said, my dad was eighty-seven years old, and he knew his time on earth was of the essence. It was so important to him that Darcy and I visit Rome. He knew we were the only ones left living that could make this trip, and he wanted to make sure his dream became a reality for us. That's why I made that promise to him, and it was a vow I was going to keep.

In March of that year, six months before our trip, I had this urge, a desire, a feeling of anxiety to write a letter to the Roman Catholic Consulate at the Vatican. In my letter, I explained to them our life and our story, of all the illnesses that affected our family, and how it was my father's dream to visit one day. I explained our marriage and how God always had an impact on our lives. I went into detail how we both received all of our sacraments from the Catholic Church, being happily married and celebrating our thirty-fifth wedding anniversary there.

In my heart I knew this letter was a long shot because they get so many of these requests from all over the world, year in and year out. But I figured, what could they say, no? I just wanted to give it a try.

Then one day I got a letter in the mail. It was from the Vatican. As I opened it up, my hands were trembling, not knowing the outcome of their decision. When I started to read it, tears were streaming down my face and my blurred vision made it difficult to read.

Miraculously, the request was approved, and the date was set. An overwhelming joy came over me like I can't even begin to explain, we were on our way to Italy and would be getting our marriage blessed on the altar at Saint Peter's Basilica! Praise God in Heaven, our dream and my dad's dream, is coming true.

At a Sunday mass in September, on a beautiful day in Rome, Italy, our dream and my father's wishes came true. We actually felt God was present with us on the altar that day, celebrating a marriage that He put together.

We thought of how proud our families would of been if they were physically there, but we knew they were there in spirit. It was an overwhelming moment. A trip of a lifetime.

While we were visiting, we made sure to take the experience to another level and visit other holy places like, the Church of San Pietro in Vincoli where we saw St. Peter's chains. The chains are actually encased in a gold and glass display on an altar in the basement of the church.

Another holy place we visited of course, was the Sistine Chapel. The breath taking murals on the ceiling painted by Michelangelo were exquisite.

One day while we were just walking and taking in the sites, a Priest happened to walk by us. As we both nodded, hello, I quickly turned to him and asked, "Father, we are looking for the Holy Stairs where Jesus Christ walked to His crucifixion, could you tell us where they might be?"

He responded to me in Italian. Of course, needless to say, we didn't understand Italian so we had no idea what he was saying. But fortunately for us, he figured that out and he pointed to the location of the Holy Stairs. We thanked him for his help, he gave us a blessing and we proceeded to walk there.

Across the Holy Stairs we noticed a hexagon looking building and we were curious about what it was.

Upon entering the building, we discovered it was a church, moreover it was Constantine's Baptistery. Inside, there were six altars. We then hear a beautiful sound coming from one of the altars in the church. It was a choir and the five o'clock Latin mass was presently in progress. Darcy and I looked at each other and agreed to enter for mass.

On the way in, I turn to Darcy and said, "How awesome would it be to get our marriage blessed by the priest here!"

After receiving Holy Communion and the final prayer was said, we then went to meet the priest in the back of the church. Walking the center aisle to the back, I remember jokingly saying to Darcy, "We may get blessed but we're going to have no idea what this Latin Catholic priest will be saying to us!" We both laughed and said, let's do it anyway.

I immediately approach the priest who served the mass and said to him, "Father, my name is Tony, and it would be an honor to have you bless our marriage even if it is in Latin, could you do that for us?"

I was using hand gestures to communicate with him, since I didn't know any Latin. He looked at me in a peculiar way and started to laugh. I was getting ready to ask again, only a little bit slower so he could understand when he interrupted me and said, "Tony, is that your name? You don't need to ask me again, I'm from Los Angeles. Of course I will bless your marriage."

Stunned in amazement, we couldn't help but laugh. For the next few minutes we were all sharing our life story and how blessed we were just to be there.

Who would of thought two twenty year old kids from New Jersey who lost most of their family by the time they were forty years old, fighting cancer, and a hearing impaired daughter would be here experiencing and living our dreams in Italy. It was a story book reality in our marriage and an event we will never, ever forget as long as we live.

But wait, we couldn't stop celebrating our marriage there. After all, no marriage vow is complete, unless you visit where your family arrived once they left Italy, so a trip to New York and St. Patrick's Cathedral in New York City was on the agenda.

Prior to leaving for our trip, I called St. Patrick's church office and spoke to Father Sanchez. We had an amazing conversation and I told him all about our life story. He felt so honored that we wanted to renew our vows on the altar of St. Patrick's, and he wanted to preside over the mass himself.

He made it an easy decision for us to board a flight and leave for New York City to meet him.

On Sunday morning, we arrived at St. Patrick's at nine forty-five a.m. to meet him in the back of the church.

It was a beautiful mass and after Father Sanchez finished his homily, he called Darcy and I to join him on the altar.

I remember when I was on the altar with him, just before our vows were being renewed, I turned to him and said quietly, "Father Sanchez, this is such a privilege for us to have you bless our marriage at St. Patrick's. We are in awe of our surroundings."

At that time, Father Sanchez turned his microphone on and while pointing and waving his hands at the congregation said, "Tony, Darcy, look at this church out there, look at the people, they are going to witness two people who have loved each other happily for thirty-five years renew their vows. It is myself, and these people here in church right now, who are in awe and honored to have you both here." Then, he smiled at us and said, "Now let's get you two married again!"

After renewing our vows that day from Father Sanchez, it was undeniably the same feeling we had when our vows were renewed at St. Peter's Basilica in Italy. God was there again for us that day too.

After mass we met with Father Sanchez for the last time, and the first thing out of his mouth was, "I want to see you both back here for your fiftieth!"

I said, "Father Sanchez, God willing, it will be an honor for us to come back here to renew our vows then too!"

With our New York trip a success, we were now on our way back home to Florida. This time on our agenda, it was time to receive our final marriage blessing in our home parish, St. Peter's in Deland.

Father Thomas Connery performed the blessing of our thirty-fifth wedding anniversary by renewing our vows. It was a subtle, but sacred mass. It was our home parish, with our home Priest and we felt the need to celebrate our marriage one last time in front of our home congregation with our children and grandchildren present.

Again, once more, we felt the presence of God.

Our journey of faith, blessings and celebration was now complete. We traveled to our roots, at St. Peter's Basilica in Rome, Italy to where our family arrived at St. Patrick's Cathedral in New York. And finally to where we presently attend mass every Sunday of our life at St. Peters in Deland, Florida.

We then took an account of our entire experience and when our marital blessings were completed we looked back and reflected.

Our thoughts were confirmed like the day we were married. Our firm belief is, if you are missing God in your marriage, go to church and pray, because you will never have a fulfilling marriage.

If you are missing God in your life, pray that He enters it, or you will never have a fulfilling life.

If you are missing God on the last days of your life on earth, pray for forgiveness and have faith and believe, and He will raise you into his heavenly kingdom for eternity.

This is our belief, this is our story, this is our truth. We have witnessed the miracles of God at work in our lives.

For you, I hope and pray that somewhere in this book you can benefit in some way by our life experiences, our failures, and our successes. I hope and pray when you read it, it leads you to a more personal relationship with God. I hope and pray most importantly, God blesses you abundantly and gives you comfort, hope and strength in your time of need.

Finally, I pray for you to find peace and happiness in your life, in your heart, and in your mind and soul. And just maybe someday, we will all have peace on earth.

Why I Wrote This Book

God, Family, Giving Back

After writing this book, at fifty-eight years old, I found myself sitting, thinking and still learning. One would think with all these experiences, I should of figured life out by now. However, in reality, there's always something to learn about people, and yourself.

My job was to share my story, openly, honestly, and compassionately with you. Life's problems are very complicated and difficult to balance. That is what I have continuously concentrated on in this book. It's like a pendulum, if problems start to swing heavily to one side, you start to feel the effects immediately. Car problems, financial distress, relationships, and family issues all become stressful at times. If you notice any one of these simple issues becoming a nuisance to you, you must try to fix it immediately. Procrastination should never be an option.

Now, that doesn't mean you can fix everything, but I have never seen anyone criticized for trying. A valiant effort, is better than none at all.

With Darcy and I, the concept of responsibility was forced upon us at an early age. Losing family so young made us appreciate our relationship, our kids, our pets, our friends, our jobs, and most of all, our God. My most heartfelt feeling I have is, *the value of a person is more valuable than anything on the face of this earth.* No job promotion, no trophy, no event you won, no piece of furniture, or car and no amount of money can ever replace that. Material wants and needs are the things we all get roped into, and the more we allow it, the more we compromise ourselves. Once we compromise ourselves, our own self worth depreciates. I ask then, what is our value to others?

The significance of God in your life is so important. To many lives are being destroyed for reasons that don't make any sense. Which leads me to this one final and most important thing I have said. Love each other as God has always taught us. It's the one simple commandment to live by, spoken out of God's own mouth. So love your life, love each other, and most importantly, love our God.

Please say a prayer for the many lives that were taken from cancer, and the lives right now that are being affected by it. And pray for the hearing impaired, May we all be able to hear the word of the Lord when He speaks. And may God answer your prayers and bless you abundantly. Stay strong, stay faithful, and love everyone.

In Loving Memory

Christine E. Cimino

Anthony L. Cimino

Mary C. Cimino

Thomas A. Cimino

Carol Flynn Cimino

Frances T. Easterling

Michele Easterling Bode

Kathryn A. Easterling

Lenny Bode

John Guinco

Al Nubby Napolitano

Robert Temple

Made in the USA
Columbia, SC
28 June 2018